THE YARRA VALLEY

& SURROUNDS

Kornelia Freeman & Ulo Pukk

M

MELBOURNE BOOKS

Portraits of
VICTORIA

The Dandenong Ranges

Legend

	Water body
	Parkland
	Major Road
	Secondary Road
	Minor Road
	Walking Trail
	Creek
	Railway
	Point of Interest
	Inaccessible Point of Interest
	Railway Station
	Township

Australia

Melbourne ••The Yarra Valley

Published by Melbourne Books
Level 9, 100 Collins Street,
Melbourne, VIC 3000
Australia
www.melbournebooks.com.au
info@melbournebooks.com.au

Disclaimer:
The authors and publisher have used their best efforts
to ensure the information presented is as accurate as
possible, but accept no responsibility with respect
to accuracy or completeness of the contents of this
book. They accept no responsibility for any loss,
inconvenience or injury incurred by any person using
this book, or by any business, individual or organisation
featured in this book.

NATIONAL LIBRARY OF AUSTRALIA
CATALOGUING-IN-PUBLICATION ENTRY:
AUTHORS: Freeman, Kornelia. Pukk, Ulo
TITLE: The Yarra Valley & Surrounds
ISBN: 9781922129000 (hbk.)
SUBJECTS: Yarra Valley Region (Vic.)–Description
and travel-Pictorial works.
Dandenong Ranges (Vic.)–History–Pictorial works.
DEWEY NUMBER: 919.452
Book design: Ning Xue, Melbourne Books

Visit the website: www.portraitsofvictoria.com.au

Portraits of
VICTORIA

May you be inspired
to explore the world created for you.

CONTENTS

INTRODUCTION

The Yarra is a river of great significance for Melbourne. The first European to appreciate the beauty of its crystal-clear water was Charles Grimes, the then acting Surveyor General of New South Wales, who in 1803 named the river Freshwater River and proclaimed the valley 'the most eligible place for a settlement that I have seen'.

Originally called *Birrarung*, meaning 'river of mists and shadows' in the Woiwurrung language, it was later named after the term *Yarra Yarra* meaning 'waterfall'. Flowing from its source in the Upper Yarra Valley for 242 kilometres, the river winds westward, eventually into Port Phillip Bay.

The Yarra Valley was Victoria's first winegrowing district. Vines were first planted in 1838 and the Yarra Valley became a premier wine-producing area for over 80 years. Wine production ceased in 1921 due to demand for fortified wines and beer instead of table wines, and with the 1930s Depression every vineyard returned to farming land. Replanting then began in the 1960s, with the area recognised as one of Australia's foremost cool-climate wine producers. Today, over 80 Yarra Valley wineries represent the area's international reputation for premium quality wine.

I have learnt how it feels to be a bird.
I have flown. Yes I have flown.
I am still astonished at it, still deeply moved.

Le Figaro, 1908

9

The early years of settlement in the Yarra Valley saw enormous pastoral runs provide land for cattle and sheep. The 1844 flood, one of a number of massive floods in Melbourne, saw the Yarra River rise 30 metres at Dights Falls. This occurrence interested surveyor Robert Hoddle, who organised an expedition and successfully located the source of the Yarra River. Hoddle's exploration paved the way for farming communities to be established. Historic Gulf Station and Yeringberg are classic examples of early pioneer settlements.

In the early 1850s gold was discovered at Warrandyte, Bendigo and Ballarat then, in 1859, in the Upper Yarra Valley, sparking gold rushes and vast population increases along the Yarra until the early 1900s. In 1861, spectacular quartz reefs were discovered at Woods Point and alluvial gold in the Jordan Valley. In 1862, the Yarra Track was opened, traversing from Melbourne via Healesville, Fernshaw, the Black Spur, Marysville and Matlock to the goldfields, encouraging entrepreneurs to offer provisions for gold prospectors.

After the gold rushes, timber cutting, sawmills and timber tramways followed. The Upper Yarra Valley forest was the largest producer of timber in Victoria, with over 200 timber mills in the 1920s.

The introduction of the railway to Healesville in 1889 and to Warburton in 1901 started a tourism boom, with tourists visiting and staying in guesthouses. Over 70 guesthouses were established around Healesville and many more in Warburton. Tourists would make the arduous journey to enjoy the beauty of the forest and the fresh mountain air.

Many famous Australians lived in the Yarra Valley including world-renowned opera singer Dame Nellie Melba, poet and writer C. J. Dennis, inventors John and Joseph Furphy, photographers John William Lindt and Nicholas Caire, artists Theodore Penleigh Boyd and Arthur Streeton, and many others. Baron Sir Ferdinand von Mueller, esteemed botanist and director of the Royal Botanic Gardens, had significant input into a number of heritage-listed gardens. William Guilfoyle, Baron von Mueller's successor, also involved himself with gardens in the Yarra Valley.

The Yarra Valley surrounds the river with many remarkable forests and views. The tall Mountain Ash of the Black Spur, the cool rainforest of Toolangi with its special walks, the magnificent Ada Tree and the views from Mount St Leonard and Mount Donna Buang, are breathtaking.

There are a wide range of attractions — from the famous Healesville Sanctuary, the early pioneer farm Gulf Station, hot air balloon rides and the Singing Gardens of C. J. Dennis at Toolangi, to Bruno's Art & Sculpture Garden in Marysville, the picturesque Alowyn Gardens at Yarra Glen, the beautiful Blue Lotus Water Garden near Warburton, a walk back in time at the Upper Yarra Museum, and the many award-winning wineries. Little-known places of beauty include the giant Californian Redwoods on the Warburton River walk, Marysville's Lady Talbot Drive and Platts Falls.

The beautiful Yarra Valley and surrounding areas — with its misty mornings, vineyards of gold, giant trees and unique attractions — is a place of wonder and inspiration.

The Yarra River winds its way through the Yarra Valley

ACHERON

The discovery of gold in the Acheron River in 1870 led to the establishment of the town. Acheron was originally known as Acheron Lower, while Acheron Upper is today known as Taggerty. Acheron is named after the Acheron River. In the 1820s, attempts were made to control squatting by issuing grazing leases. The Acheron Run was 9712 hectares and Acheron Station was a place for travellers to rest. One of those who stopped by was Eugene von Guérard (1811–1901), who painted *Valley of the Acheron River* in 1863.

Mechanics Institute

The Acheron Hall was built in 1914 by Mr J. Ferguson

Breakaway Bridge

The first bridge was built in 1877 but was swept away in a flood around 1918. The single-lane trestle bridge crosses the Goulburn River and was built in 1920. The river 'broke away' and formed a new course in 1932.

Two Rivers Green Tea Plantation

Two Rivers Green Tea Plantation is located on the fertile river flats where the Acheron and Goulburn rivers meet in the Acheron Valley. William and Georgie Leckey grow over 12 hectares of green tea for Australia and Japan. The 170,000 *Camellia sinensis* were planted in 2001 and include three varieties: *sayamakaori, yabukita* and *okuhikaori*.

Heatherly Homestead

Heatherly is the 1920s homestead of the Leckey family, who have owned the property for 40 years. Over 150 varieties of roses grow in the garden. Chinese Wisteria and an ornamental grapevine adorn the tennis pavilion.

THE BLACK SPUR

The Black Spur is the area on the Maroondah Highway between Healesville and Narbethong. It was once known as The Blacks' Spur, as it was the track used by Aboriginals through the Great Dividing Range. In the 1870s, red Cobb and Co. coaches ran a daily service from Bourke Street in Melbourne's CBD to Marysville. The Blacks' Spur was a popular tourist destination for people, including famous photographers Nicholas Caire and John William Lindt, who valued its scenic beauty.

Boat O'Craigo

The Boat O'Craigo name comes from the town of Craigo, in Scotland. The boutique winery produces outstanding wines of many different varieties.

Saint Ronan's Well

Saint Ronan's Well is an early watering point used by bullock teams and horses travelling along the Black Spur. When travelling in the past, rest stops and the provision of water was important. The water comes from a natural mountain spring and is collected into a small well. The old Blacks' Spur road meets the Maroondah Highway at Saint Ronan's Well.

Graceburn Weir

Graceburn Weir and its aqueduct were built in 1891 to divert water from Graceburn Creek, collecting water between Mount Juliet and Mount Riddell into the Maroondah Reservoir.

Water from the aqueduct enters the reservoir at the 'Bubble Hole', an exposed section of riveted iron pipe. The name Bubble Hole describes the surge of water from the aqueduct, which has been a popular place since the opening of the reservoir in 1927.

The walk to Graceburn Weir from the Maroondah Highway is a three-kilometre return trip.

Those who contemplate the beauty of the earth find reserves of strength that will endure as long as life lasts.
Rachel Carson (1907–1964)

Fernshaw Park

Fernshaw is the site of an 1860s township located near the start of the Black Spur, an early route for travellers to the Woods Point goldfields. Its residents were teamsters, road makers, timber splitters and fruit growers. In the 1880s, the Water Supply Board decided to reserve the Watts River area for Melbourne's water supply. Between 1885 and 1890, land in the Maroondah Catchment was purchased by the government and the buildings in Fernshaw were removed or demolished.

Famous photographer Nicholas Caire (1837–1918), described the site as

a veritable nest of fairy fern glen, nothing like it being known in the wide world, except perhaps the Himalayas.

The reserve contains magnificent sequoia, cork oak and other trees.

BOTTOM LEFT
The reserve features an oak tree with a plaque commemorating the visit in 1901 by Queen Mary, then Duchess of York, consort of King George V. The tree was cultivated from an acorn taken from one of William the Conqueror's oak trees at Windsor Castle.

BOTTOM RIGHT
Fernshaw Reserve is a grassed area on the banks of the Watts River

Halcyon – Private Garden

Originally, the property was the Brockenhurst Guesthouse, which burnt down in 1926. Dr Karl Stephens then acquired the property, constructed the house and landscaped the garden. A number of large trees date from the late 1920s. Later, in the 1940s, hydrangeas, azaleas and rhododendrons were planted. A truly beautiful old 1.6-hectare garden, it is rarely opened to the public and incorporates a parterre, walled vegetable garden, several dry-stone walls, rose garden, sweeping lawns and a huge variety of very old European trees. Halcyon has been in the same family since the 1940s and is part of a 40-hectare farm.

What if you have seen it before,
ten thousand times over?
An apple tree in full blossom is
like a message,
sent fresh from heaven to earth,
of purity and beauty.

Henry Ward Beecher (1813–1887)

Maroondah Reservoir Park

The Maroondah Reservoir is part of the water catchment area for Melbourne's water supply. Dam construction started in 1920 and was completed in 1927. The dam wall is 41 metres high and the reservoir has a capacity of 22,000 megalitres. Many exotic plants are included in the landscaped parkland.

LEFT
The Rose Steps lead from the base of the Maroondah dam wall

RIGHT TOP
The overflow spillway channels water over the rocky outlet

RIGHT BOTTOM
The view from the top of the dam wall, showing historic valve houses, the lily pond, MMBW sundial and curved Compensation Channel

Condon's Gully

Condon's Gully was an early popular walk and inspired the noted photographer Nicholas Caire to describe it as 'the most beautiful and romantic gully in the district'. Another noted photographer, John William Lindt (1845–1926), who lived nearby at The Hermitage, described it as 'the fern gully of all fern gullies'. The track to what was once Condon's Picnic Ground is open and continues along to Mount Monda.

TOP LEFT
Condon's Track meanders to Echo Point, with beautiful specimens of giant Sequoia

Mathinna Falls

A beautiful series of three falls on Mount Monda, the Mathinna Falls are now closed to the public. With the construction of the Maroondah Weir in 1891, the fern gullies and waterfalls in the Maroondah Catchment were popular with tourists.

Rose Stereograph Co. (1920–1954), Pictures Collection, State Library of Victoria

Furmston's Trees

Harold Furmston and his brother Ron discovered two magnificent Mountain Ash trees on Mount Monda. Harold's tree is likely the same as that spotted by Baron Ferdinand von Mueller in the 1850s. A popular walk for tourists in the early 1900s began from Fernshaw, proceeding to the Mathinna Falls and to Harold Furmston's giant tree. Access to the tree is no longer allowed, and it is believed to have fallen. The huge tree had a girth of 19.5 metres.

Morwell Hodges (1914–1941), A. C. Dreier Postcard Collection, Pictures Collection, State Library of Victoria

Mount Dom Dom
Picnic Ground

The conical shape of Mount Dom Dom can be seen from the picnic ground at Mount Dom Dom Saddle. The peak has an altitude of 732 metres.

LEFT
The road along the Black Spur displays what is regarded as some of the most beautiful scenery of tall Mountain Ash and ferns.

RIGHT
Historic drinking fountain

Mount Juliet

Mount Juliet was named after the daughter of Anne and Colonel Joseph Anderson (1790–1877). Juliet's sister, Lilly, married vigneron Paul De Castella.

The walk to the Mount Juliet summit is very steep, with the walking trail rising over 900 metres and the peak reaching 1105 metres above sea level. The mountain was first climbed in the 1850s by a group of Royal Engineers (or 'Sappers') to establish a survey trigonometry station.

In 1862, James Murphy, a mining surveyor. aspired to make a track from Mount Juliet to the Jordan Valley goldfields. The track was so steep that Thomas Guerin, the government surveyor at the time, decided instead to establish the route through the Black Spur.

Until around 1860, Mount Juliet was considered the highest in the range. Magistrate Joseph Panton (1831–1913) mapped the Yarra Valley and found that Mount Donna Buang was about 100 metres higher.

The Grade 4 walking track starts where May Town was once situated, near Mosquito Creek. The track shown above starts at the Maroondah Highway.

The Mount Juliet cairn is associated with the first Victorian geodetic survey, conducted between 1858 and 1872. It is regarded as the best preserved of the dry-stone survey cairns, and is 5.5 metres high and 4.6 metres in diameter. Mount Juliet was a popular destination for walkers visiting the Healesville area in the early 1900s.

Narbethong

For centuries, the Tuanarong people travelled from the Narbethong area to the Healesville area to conduct ceremonies, marry and trade with neighbouring clans. Narbethong was also a rest place for prospectors on the way to the Woods Point, Enochs Point and Jamieson goldfields. The name Narbethong comes from the Tuanarong words *Naah Naah Thong*, meaning 'a cheerful place'. It was named by surveyor John Wrigglesworth in 1865.

The Hermitage Guesthouse

The Hermitage is an historic guesthouse on a 32-hectare site, built in 1894 by German-born photographer John William Lindt. Lindt arrived in Australia in 1862 and worked as a successful photographer in Grafton. He then moved to Melbourne in 1876, opening a studio on Collins Street.

TOP

A lichgate consists of a roofed structure over a gate. The Hermitage's lichgate has picket gates, lattice work and a seat, and was a landmark denoting the northern end of the Black Spur. The driveway was originally part of the Maroondah Highway. J. W. Lindt, c. 1920, Pictures Collection, State Library of Victoria

BOTTOM

The Hermitage was built as a pleasure resort for the rich and famous. Its guests include Lady Stanley, the wife of Sir Arthur Stanley (former governor of Victoria); The Royal Geographical Society; Baron Ferdinand von Mueller; and renowned opera singer Dame Nellie Melba.

Following the 1890s financial crash, Lindt closed his business and built The Hermitage. The property included a main residence, guesthouse, studio, a smokers' cottage, bachelors' quarters, fountain, rotunda, pool, three tree houses, a lake, a natural spring and walking tracks into the forest. Current owners Joe and Maryanne Messina continue to run The Hermitage as a guesthouse.

The Smokers' Cottage has outside walls made from wooden shingles. The buildings on the estate were built in the style of a Swiss chalet. Lindt was the architect and Pomeroy, from Healesville, was the builder.

The studio was originally a church built in England, which Lindt bought for use as his photographic studio in Hawthorn and later moved to Narbethong.

A giant Mountain Grey Gum (*Eucalyptus cypellocarpa*) of approximately 12 metres girth is located in the forest at The Hermitage.

Lindt built three tree houses in the largest trees. He was inspired by his trip to New Guinea and would photograph his estate from the tree houses in every season.

The garden also includes Silver Birches, Japanese Cedar, Italian Cypress, Himalayan Cedar, Linden, Sierra Redwood, Coast Redwood, chestnut, azaleas and rhododendrons.

Ferns surround the tranquil lake

Old Blacks' Spur Road

The old Blacks' Spur Road was a major road for travellers to the Woods Point and Jamieson goldfields, and later for excursionists travelling to Healesville or Marysville.

The original route to the goldfields was via Mansfield and Jamieson, a journey of 350 kilometres. In 1862, a better alternative, the Yarra Track, was explored, reducing the route to 160 kilometres. Construction of the Yarra Track started in 1863. It ran from Healesville, through the Watts River valley to The Blacks' Spur, then through the Acheron Valley to Marysville. In 1874, Cobb and Co. coaches travelled along the Yarra Track from Melbourne to Woods Point.

The seven-kilometre-long old Blacks' Spur Road contains historic sites but most is now part of the inaccessible Maroondah Catchment. The new highway route was built in 1937 to 1938.

The giant, old tree stump, located near the old Blacks' Spur Road, shows the deep cuts where tree fallers fitted boards to stand on, so they could cut above the wide buttress of the giant Mountain Ash.

Bunyip State Park

The first people to live in the area were the Balluk-willam clan of the Woiwurrung (Yarra Yarra) Aboriginal people. Prospectors were the first Europeans to visit the district in the mid-1850s. The Bunyip State Park area became popular for its timber. The name comes from the Aboriginal word *Bunyip* or *Buneep*, referring to a monstrous swamp-dwelling creature. Local Aboriginal people believed the Bunyip lived in the swamps of the Bunyip River and avoided the area; thus, many early settlers also did not camp near the 'Bunyip Hole'. The park is 16,000 hectares in size.

As superintendent of the Port Phillip District in 1847, Charles La Trobe wrote of the constant rumours of 'some unknown beast'. Various Kulin provided him sketches of a large billabong- and river-based creature resembling a plesiosaurus. There were also sightings at Tooradin.

Egg Rock and Fire Tower

The rock slopes and boulders at Egg Rock are outcrops of Tynong Granite.

Four Brothers Rocks

The rocks are the highest point of the Black Snake Range, at 420 metres above sea level.

Most of the mysteries of the once mysterious Australian continent are mysteries no longer, but at least one - perhaps the most fascinating of all - remains. It is the Bunyip.

C. D. Brammall (1958)

BUXTON

The town of Buxton is located on the foothills of the magnificent Cathedral Range. The Acheron River cascades through Buxton, which is famous for its trout-fishing. John and James Thomson were the first white settlers in 1866. By the 1870s, the settlement had grown to a town. Oats were grown to feed the horses carrying supplies to the Woods Point goldfields. Buxton is a popular place for people seeking peaceful surroundings and excellent trout fishing.

Buxton Ridge

Buxton Ridge wines are handmade using traditional methods including hand-plunging in open fermenters and gentle basket-pressing. Pinot, Merlot, Shiraz, Sauvignon Blanc and a Sparkling Pinot are made at the vineyard. Their award-winning wines also are available at the cellar door.

Buxton Silver Gum Reserve

The Buxton Gum (*Eucalyptus crenulata*) is a tree that grows to eight metres in height. It has small leaves that are glaucous (blue-green in colour with a surface of white wax particles). It is endemic to Victoria, with only two natural populations: 600 trees at the Buxton Silver Gum Reserve, and 15 trees at the floodplain of the Yarra River at Yering. The reserve was set aside in 1978.

Buxton Trout & Salmon Farm

Australia's first commercial trout hatchery, established in 1958, grows quality Rainbow Trout and Atlantic Salmon in the pristine waters of the Victorian Alps. There are a variety of ponds for large trout (0.5–3 kilograms), medium trout (0.3–0.5 kilograms) and salmon, as well as a challenge lake.

Seal Rock

Cathedral Range State Park

The Cathedral Range is a spectacular seven-kilometre ridge of upturned sedimentary rock, located nine kilometres north-east of Buxton. From the mountain, beautiful views can be seen across the Acheron Valley. The mountain range has steep sides with a narrow razorback ridge between the Jawbones and Mount Sugarloaf. The east plateau continues to Lake Mountain.

The view looking north, along the razorback ridge, from Mount Sugarloaf

Steep climbs are typical of the mountain terrain.

Koala (*Phascolarctos cinereus*). The park is home to lyrebirds, Satin bowerbirds, koalas, kangaroos and wombats.

Looking south towards the South Jawbones peak and Mount Sugarloaf

CHRISTMAS HILLS

The Christmas Hills area was part of the land occupied by the Eaglehawk and the Crow people of the Wurundjeri. It is very hilly, with One Tree Hill in the north-west rising to 372 metres above sea level.

In the 1840s, European settlers moved along the Yarra River with sheep and cattle and settled here. Victoria's first officially recognised gold find was in 1851 at Anderson's Creek in Warrandyte, ten kilometres from Sugarloaf Hill. Gold was discovered at One Tree Hill in 1859 with quartz reef mining continuing until 1864, and alluvial mining to 1908. The Wurundjeri population declined and Christmas Hills became established as a farming community.

Sugarloaf Reservoir

In the late 1970s, construction began on a dam across Sugarloaf Creek, which was completed in 1980. With a capacity of 95,000 megalitres, it supplies Melbourne with water. The reservoir receives water from the Maroondah aqueduct as well as water pumped from the Yarra River at Yering Gorge.

Around the reservoir is Sugarloaf Reservoir Park, opened in 1982 and home to Eastern Grey Kangaroos and echidnas.

David Christmas

A Welshman born in 1797 in Cardiganshire, David Christmas was transported to Van Diemen's Land in 1822 for the term of his natural life and was granted a free pardon in 1829. Joseph Stevenson hired David in 1842 to be a shepherd to his animals, which were in pasture around the valleys of the Watson and Sugarloaf creeks.

The camp was a 45-kilometre walk from Melbourne, with a large part through trackless bush. David became lost and after wandering for a considerable time, was weak and exhausted. Hearing the distant sound of a bullock bell, David struggled to the direction of the bell. Joseph Stevenson had come to herd his cattle and found David.

The cattle run was named Christmas Hill Station, which was later adopted by the rural community.

Bend of Islands, Yarra River

COLDSTREAM

The Coldstream township was originally known as The Lodge. In 1859, Kerr and Robert Black named their estate Coldstream after a place on the border between England and Scotland. Coldstream developed around the railway station, which was established in 1888. In 1909, Dame Nellie Melba bought Coombe Cottage at Coldstream. The neighbouring Melba Highway is named in her honour.

The area is known for farming and winemaking.

Coombe Cottage

In 1909, Melba bought a 24-hectare property with a small home at Coldstream. Around 1912 she had Coombe Cottage built, naming it after a home she rented in England.

Coombe Cottage is a private residence and is not normally open to the public.

Maroondah Orchards

Maroondah Orchards are growers and retailers of apples, peaches, nectarines and pears.

Beef cattle, strawberries, orchards and sheep farms are located in the area

Badger's Brook Estate

Established in 1993, Badger's Brook Estate specialises in Chardonnay, Pinot Noir and Shiraz. The wines are made from low yielding vines on the property and with fruit from selected growers. Badger's Brook wines are made for cellaring, while their Storm Ridge wines are made for more immediate consumption.

Dame Nellie Melba

Dame Nellie Melba (1861–1931) was born Helen Porter Mitchell to a musical family in the Melbourne suburb of Richmond. Her Scottish father, David Mitchell, was a building contractor and a bass vocalist, and her mother, Isabella, was her first music teacher. Her mother died in 1881, followed by her youngest sister.

Melba's pure lyrical voice and brilliant technique was the reason she was called 'the world's greatest singer'. Melba was the first Australian to achieve international recognition as a classical musician. Following appearances in Sydney and London, she made her operatic debut in Brussels in 1887. It was the start of a 38-year career on the world stage. She adopted the professional name *Melba* to acknowledge her birthplace, Melbourne.

Melba won acclaim at Covent Garden, London, and sang at most of the leading opera houses of the world, including the Metropolitan Opera, New York; La Scala; the Imperial Opera, St Petersburg; and with Caruso in Monte Carlo. She was the epitome of fame and glamour.

Melba's triumphant homecoming in 1902 involved a concert tour of Australia and New Zealand. Wherever she travelled, large crowds greeted her. Melba made her first commercial recordings in 1904. She released over 100 records and helped to establish the gramophone. In 1909, Melba went on a 'sentimental tour' of Australia and was welcomed warmly in every town she visited.

She bought property at Coldstream and around 1912 had Coombe Cottage built. Melba loved entertaining and Coombe was often crowded with guests. Melba set up a music school in Richmond, which later merged into the Melbourne Conservatorium. When war broke out she raised money for war charities, giving dozens of concerts, for which she sang without fee, and raising over £100,000 — a huge sum in those days. Melba was appointed a Dame of the British Empire in 1918 and a Dame Grand Cross in 1927.

In 1920, she was the first artist of international standing to participate in direct radio broadcasts. In 1928 Melba held her last local performance before visiting Europe. She returned to Sydney in declining health, where she passed away. Melba was given a state funeral at Scots' Church, Melbourne, which her father built and where she had sung in the choir as a teenager. Melba is buried in the Lilydale Cemetery. Her headstone says: *Addio, senza rancor* ('Farewell, without bitterness'). Melba was the last of the 19th century's bel canto sopranos.

Pictures Collection, State Library of Victoria

Coombe Cottage Music Room, 1910–1920
Pictures Collection, State Library of Victoria

Domaine Chandon

Domaine Chandon in the Yarra Valley is a world-class winery that produces sparkling and still wines for domestic and international markets. The winery attracts over 200,000 visitors a year. In 1985, Moët and Chandon searched for the ideal location in Australia for growing traditional Champagne varieties, establishing Domaine Chandon in 1986.

Domaine Chandon has plantings of the Champagne grape varietals: Chardonnay, Pinot Noir and Pinot Meunier. Grapes are also sourced from other vineyards in Victoria, South Australia and Tasmania. The winemaking procedures are similar to those used by Moët and Chandon in France, one of the world's most famous Champagne houses, established in 1743. Chandon estates outside of France can also be found in Argentina (Bodegas Chandon, 1960), Brazil (Chandon do Brasil, 1963) and California (Domaine Chandon California, 1973).

The sun, with all those planets revolving around it and dependent on it, can still ripen a bunch of grapes as if it had nothing else in the universe to do.

Galileo Galilei (1564–1642)

Spectacular views can be enjoyed while tasting wines in The Greenpoint Brasserie Tasting Bar. It is one of the best food and wine restaurants in the Yarra Valley.

The 1880s homestead hosts wine tastings and special events

The Green Point vineyard surrounds the winery. The cool environment is influenced by the weather patterns from the Southern Ocean. The spur of land was named Green Point in the 1860s by the early settlers, who noticed that the property remained green long into the dry summer because of the soil's excellent water retention.

Dominique Portet

The Dominique Portet label began in 2000. Dominique is the ninth generation in his family committed to winemaking, with family links to the production of wine preceding 1720.

The Portet family has a commitment to high-quality winemaking of exceptional standards. The Dominique Portet winery has a Mediterranean atmosphere, with simple lunches, wine and barrel tastings, and vintage tours.

Gateway Estate

Gateway operates one of the most unique cellar doors in the Yarra Valley, positioned in a farm gate environment alongside a hydroponic greenhouse. Award-winning wines, relishes and preserves can be sampled. Also available are aged beef, local berries, apples, stone fruit, vegetables and fresh seasonal produce.

Gateway produces a range of wines that can be enjoyed by themselves or to complement lighter, fresher styles in modern food.

Helen's Hill Estate

At Helen's Hill, traditional values and modern efficiencies are used to make exceptional cool-climate wines. Comprising 60 hectares, the vineyard includes a 140-seat restaurant and some of the finest views of the Yarra Valley. Located well above the valley floor with a number of hills running through the property, the different soil types and microclimates are matched to the grape varieties, allowing them to grow to their optimum. The cellar door has events planned, from gala dinners to music festivals or family fun days. Some of the finest pâté, cheeses and antipasto platters can be enjoyed on the outdoor deck.

Maddens Rise

Maddens Rise use biological farming practices wherever practical. Wine is made on-site using hand-picked grapes, small batch fermentation, minimal oak and wild yeasts. Grapes planted include Chardonnay, Pinot Noir, Pinot Meunier, Cabernet Sauvignon, Merlot, Nebbiolo, Cabernet Franc, Petit Verdot, Shiraz, Malbec, Arneis, Chenin Blanc, Fiano, Garganega, Viognier, Vermentino and Sangiovese — introducing great variety. On the property is one of the Yarra Valley's oldest woolsheds.

Oakridge

Oakridge has been making wine in the Yarra Valley since 1978 and regularly produces wines of exemplary quality. Stretching across ten hectares of landscaped vines and gardens, the estate features a welcoming cellar door and restaurant, and is dedicated to producing outstanding and distinctive wines. The contemporary restaurant has the most stunning views, with a selection of dishes guaranteed to excite the palate. Its cuisine proudly features the produce and flavours of the Valley.

Punt Road

Punt Road Wines brings a wealth of experience and a passion for wine. Fruit is sourced from over 75 hectares of vineyards. Only small parcels of the best fruit are used. The cellar door provides a warm, friendly environment for a complete and relaxing wine-tasting experience. There is room for children to run around, a casual barbecue or a game of Pétanque.

Rochford

Rochford Winery is situated in one of the most stunning areas, with panoramic views of the Great Dividing Range. It is known for its innovative events, food and wine, and is identified with the iconic Australian 'A Day on the Green' music festivals.

The winery has a restaurant, café and patio, cellar door, retail shop, wine club, art gallery, a natural amphitheatre and observation tower. The venue can cater up to 7000 guests. The café and patio are perfect for casual lunches while looking over the vineyard.

Rochford's wines have won numerous medals and awards.

St Huberts

Hubert de Castella named the winery after his patron saint when he first established the winery in 1862. By the 1890s, it had become the largest in Australia. The vineyard was planted in 1966 on one of the best viticultural sites in the Yarra Valley. The vines are low-yield with intense fruit flavours and great depth of colour. St Huberts has a long tradition of producing distinctive Cabernet Sauvignon and Pinot Noir.

The cellar door offers tastings, coffee and wine merchandise. The shade under the winery's elm tree creates a lovely place to enjoy a cheese platter, picnic or barbecue.

Stones of the Yarra Valley

Stones of the Yarra Valley is located on one of the most picturesque and historic properties in the Yarra Valley, combining a restaurant and mezze bar with a stunning rough-rendered chapel nestled under century-old oaks.

Concerts by world-renowned artists are regularly held at The Stables at Stones. With its vintage fittings, rough-hewn timbers and century-old brickwork, it is one of the Yarra Valley's iconic heritage venues.

Tokar Estate

With majestic sweeping views of the Yarra Valley and its surrounding mountain ranges, Tokar Estate is an ideal location to relax, soak up nature's beauty, taste exquisite wines and sample exotic cuisine. The estate's cellar door has a fabulous range of boutique wines and new vintage releases, including the award-winning Tempranillo and flagship wine The Aria. The Tokar Restaurant offers magnificent Mediterranean cuisine along with spectacular views of the Yarra Valley.

Tokar Estate's 12 hectares of vines have been producing premium fruit since 1998.

DIXONS CREEK

Dixons Creek, named after former local resident
John Dixon, is a fruit-growing, grazing and wine district.
Its post office opened in 1902 and closed in 1967.

Early morning autumn mist

Allinda Winery

Established in 1990 by Al and Linda Fencaros,
Allinda Winery produces award-winning
estate-grown wines on three hectares.
The vineyard was planted with Cabernet,
Chardonnay and Riesling clones sourced from
local vineyards to produce optimum fruit quality.
Biological farming practices are used based on
the principles of Elaine Ingham.

*The rustic
cellar door is
constructed from
timber recycled
from an 1886
woolstore.*

De Bortoli Yarra Valley Estate

Vittorio De Bortoli emigrated to Australia from Northern Italy and worked hard before buying a fruit farm in New South Wales. He established De Bortoli Wines in 1928 and married his childhood sweetheart, Giuseppina, in 1929. They had three children and it was their son Deen who continued to expand the business from the 1950s. Deen and his wife, Emeri, had four children: Darren, Leanne, Kevin and Victor. Today, De Bortoli Wines is in the hands of this third generation.

The De Bortoli vineyards are located in the Riverina and Hunter Valley (New South Wales) as well as the Yarra Valley and King Valley (Victoria). Deen's son Darren created the iconic dessert wine Noble One at the Bilbul vineyard in the Riverina, and it is now one of the most awarded wines in Australian history.

The De Bortoli family purchased their Yarra Valley vineyard in 1987. Deen's daughter, Leanne, along with her husband, Stephen Webber, manage the 240-hectare estate, which produces many of the premium wines for the company.

De Bortoli Wines is one of Australia's largest wineries, exporting to more than 70 countries. It is still a family-owned company with strong values of hard work, generosity of spirit and the joy of sharing a glass of wine over good food with family and friends.

The Locale restaurant reflects the De Bortoli family's Italian heritage and sources the best local, seasonal and organic produce. To enhance the visitors' experience, a cheese room has been added to the cellar door facility, where cheese is stored in the maturation room and can be tasted and purchased by customers.

Avenue showing autumn's beauty

Semper ad Majora

('Always striving for better')

De Bortoli family motto

Classic varieties grown are Chardonnay, Sauvignon, Viognier, Pinot Noir, Cabernet Sauvignon and Shiraz.

Fergusson Winery

The Fergusson vineyard was planted by the Fergusson family in 1968 with classic French grape varieties including Chardonnay, Pinot Noir, Shiraz and Cabernet Sauvignon. Louise Fergusson is executive chef at the renowned Fergusson Restaurant and has worked at top restaurants in England, France and Germany.

RIGHT
The Vineyard Homestead accommodates groups and families in a tranquil secret garden with a magnificent antique pavilion.

FAR RIGHT
The storybook chapel nestled among the vines is very popular for weddings.

Immerse

Situated among the vines and beautiful rose gardens, away from the pressures of life, Immerse offers handcrafted wines of exceptional flavour and quality from 25-year-old vines. Sauvignon Blanc, Pinot Noir, Shiraz and Chardonnay are grown on the estate. Wine tutorials and appreciation classes; spa treatments and massages; wedding, conference and accommodation packages; golf; and gourmet restaurant meals are also available.

Mandala

Mandala is operated by Charles Smedley and is a five-star winery, as rated by James Halliday. The 20-year-old vines include Chardonnay, Shiraz, Cabernet Sauvignon and Pinot Noir, producing beautifully poised fruit. The restaurant has 180-degree views through glass-walled spaces. Mandala has one of the most stylish cellar doors in the Yarra Valley.

Miller's Dixons Creek Estate

Graeme Miller is one of the pioneers of the rebirth of the Yarra Valley as a wine region in the sixties and seventies. In 1971, he established Chateau Yarrinya, which was sold to the De Bortoli family in 1987.

Miller's Dixons Creek Estate was planted in 1988 and has produced many award-winning wines.

The vineyard covers 58 hectares with Shiraz, Cabernet Sauvignon, Cabernet Franc, Carménère, Pinot Noir, Verdot, Merlot, Chardonnay, Sauvignon Blanc and Pinot Gris. Miller's Dixons Creek Estate displays a collection of Aboriginal art from the Central and Western Desert areas.

We ought to do good to others as simply as a horse runs, or a bee makes honey, or a vine bears grapes season after season without thinking of the grapes it has borne.

Marcus Aurelius (121–180)

Shantell Vineyard & Winery

The property was purchased in 1980 by Shan and Turid Shanmugam and the first vines were planted in 1981. Ten hectares of vineyard have been planted with the premium grape varieties Chardonnay, Pinot Noir, Cabernet Sauvignon, Semillon and Shiraz, producing wines of finesse and exceptional flavour. The Shantell Cellar Door Restaurant offers a selection of fine food and wines. There are two open verandahs for outdoor dining among the vines. Fresh produce is grown in the vegetable gardens. A unique Aboriginal art collection is on display.

Sutherland Estate

Sutherland Estate is built on the side of Daniel's Hill, with spectacular views. Premium grape varieties planted in 1995 on four hectares include Chardonnay, Pinot Noir, Cabernet Sauvignon and Shiraz. Gewurztraminer and Tempranillo varieties of Spanish origin — rarities in the Yarra Valley — were planted in 2002.

The estate's 200-metre elevation allows for a longer ripening season, producing the estate's many award-winning wines of varietal intensity, elegance and complexity.

The picturesque lake and natural bushland are home to Eastern Grey Kangaroos, wombats, echidnas, Wedge-tailed Eagles, kites and magpies.

The cellar door, designed by Ron Phelan, is available for weddings and has enormous floor-to-ceiling windows. The cathedral ceiling is capped with a glass prism. Two towers frame the cellar door and provide luxurious accommodation.

Don Valley

John and Catherine Ewart arrived in Launching Place in the 1840s. Their son, David, and his wife, Annie, were the first white settlers in Don Valley, at the foot of Mount Toolebewong. David and Annie had 12 children. Their property was named Glenewart, and its 120 hectares included tribal grounds of Barak's Yarra Yarra Aboriginals, who accepted David as a tribal member. Glenewart is now managed by the Victorian Conservation Trust.

Tree ferns line the road through Don Valley, which leads to Panton's Gap. The mountain home of Magistrate Joseph Anderson Panton (1831–1913) stood above the valley.

GLENBURN

Glenburn is part of the Murrindindi Shire and is surrounded by beautiful views of hills, valleys, and sheep, dairy and beef farms. The Glenburn post office opened in 1902, when it was known as the Glenburn Creamery until 1907. Glenburn is renowned as a place to view hot air balloons rise into the early morning skies.

When you arise in the morning, think of what a precious privilege it is to be alive — to breathe, to think, to enjoy, to love.

Marcus Aurelius (121–180)

GRUYERE

Gruyere was previously known as Cahillton, until Swiss vigneron Paul de Castella suggested the name Gruyere, a variety of cheese, as the area is a farming district and wine region. Its post office opened in 1892.

Coldstream Hills

Established by James and Suzanne Halliday in 1985, Coldstream Hills has grown to be one of the Australia's leading small wineries. Coldstream Hills concentrates its efforts on three main varieties — Chardonnay, Pinot Noir and the Cabernet family — and its award-winning wines are handmade. The aim of the winemaking team at Coldstream Hills is to produce wines of elegance with a long finish.

The future belongs to those who believe in the beauty of their dreams.

Eleanor Roosevelt (1884–1962)

Medhurst Wines

Medhurst Wines aims to make the best wine possible. Careful vineyard management, ensuring low yields, provides intensely flavoured fruit. The varieties grown include Chardonnay, Sauvignon Blanc, Pinot Noir, Cabernet Sauvignon and Shiraz. Medhurst makes a Rosé from its Cabernet and Shiraz fruit. The cellar door is located on the hill looking over the vineyard. At the cellar door is the restaurant Medhurst Cellar Door & More, where delicious dishes are served.

Soumah

A passion for horticulture and wine is the driving force for making super premium wines with varietal and regional character. Soumah targets quality over quantity, as well as the production of savoury, elegant wines.

Soumah is an acronym for the location: South of Maroondah Highway. The first vintage attracted many accolades, featuring Savarro, Pinot Grigio, Viognier, Chardonnay, Shiraz and Pinot Noir.

Courtesy of Soumah

Courtesy of Soumah

Warramate Wines

Established in 1970, Warramate Wines produces premium-quality handcrafted Riesling, Cabernet Merlot, Pinot Noir and Shiraz wines. From the beginning, the vines have been 'dry-grown' (without irrigation) and pruned and harvested by hand. The Warramate philosophy is to make the highest-quality wines from excellent estate fruit in a sustainable manner.

Jack and June Church first started planting the vines in 1969. Jack searched throughout Victoria for a suitable plot for his dream vineyard and found the perfect location on the north-facing slopes of the Warramate Hills. Warramate Wines is now owned by Richard Magides and Ed Peter (This Century Pty Ltd).

Yarra Yering

Yarra Yering is one of the most beautiful vineyards in the Yarra Valley, with an international reputation for quality and individuality.

In 1969, after a long search for the perfect site, Dr Bailey Carrodus planted 12 hectares of vines at the foot of the Warramate Hills. The gentle slope, with its northerly aspect, has good drainage, all-day exposure to the sun, and enough elevation from the valley floor to avoid the spring frosts. The vineyard was named Yarra Yering, and in 1973 it produced the first commercial vintage of wine from the Yarra Valley since 1923.

In 2011, Carrodus was bestowed a posthumous honour by his old college, Queens, at Oxford University. The refurbished Queens Lane Quad, a 70-room accommodation building, was renamed Carrodus Quad in his memory. During his time at Oxford he acquired a love for the sophisticated wines of Europe, and it is this love that inspired him to establish Yarra Yering.

Warramate Hills

The Warramate Hills Flora and Fauna Reserve is located in the Warramate Hills, which consists of two peaks: Briarty Hill (420 metres) and Steel Hill (395 metres). Robert Briarty, an early selector in the 1850s, established the Steel's Flat run along the Wandin Yallock Creek valley.

From the hilltops, visitors can enjoy panoramic views of where the slopes were cleared of native vegetation in the 1960s.

HEALESVILLE

Healesville is located at the junction of the Graceburn and Watts rivers in the foothills of the Great Dividing Range. Around 1860, the Yarra Track to the booming Woods Point goldfield was established. The track led from the Diamond Valley, across the Watts River to the north of Healesville, through the settlement known as New Chum Creek which had lodging houses, a blacksmith and a mining warden's office.

In 1863, a new road was constructed to the south of New Chum Creek. It passed through a new town that was surveyed in 1864 and named Healesville in honour of Richard Heales, the Victorian premier from 1860 to 1861, who had died that year. New Chum Creek was abandoned and Healesville flourished, offering hospitality to the passing traffic of prospectors and timber-cutters.

Traffic to the goldfields declined in the 1870s. Some miners settled in Healesville, turning to farming and growing fruit and hops.

In the 1880s, tourists came to see the fern gullies, mountains and giant trees that were popularised by the photographs of Nicholas Caire and John William Lindt. When the railway line was constructed in 1889, Healesville had a tourist focus, with grand hotels and guesthouses including the 60-room Gracedale House (1889) overlooking Maroondah Dam, which operated until the 1950s.

River Street

One might regard architecture as history arrested in stone.

A.L. Rowse (1903 – 1997)

Healesville has many heritage buildings,
with old-style architectural beauty.

Artspace & Palette

Artspace & Palette showcases the best local and international contemporary art and delicious food.

Court House

The old Court House was built in 1890 and closed in 1990. It is now used as the Yarra Valley Tourist Information Centre.

Rathrone House

Established in 1886, it was named after the birthplace of the owner, Constable Tevlin, in Ireland.

Healesville Hotel

The hotel was rebuilt in 1912.

Old Gaol Cells

The cell blocks were built in 1866.

Grand Hotel

Built by Adolphus Edgecumbe in the French Second Empire style in 1888. The architect was Walter Pitt, designer of the Princess Theatre in Melbourne.

Former Mechanics Institute and Free Library

Built in 1892, it was a library until 1924. Since 1930 it had auction rooms and served as a doctor's surgery, photographic studio, gallery and tea rooms.

The Nook

In 1866, Mr Hetherton established a house near the Graceburn River. Pictured is an historic fountain, now a memorial for soldiers. The Nook is part of Queens Park.

Mt Yule

The Mt Yule property once belonged to William Guilfoyle (1840–1912), who was Director of Melbourne's Royal Botanic Gardens from 1873 to 1909. The nine-hectare property in River Street was his country home. Subtropical vegetation was a trademark of a Guilfoyle garden.

Mt Riddell

The old stone cairn marks the top of Mt Riddell, which rises from 200 metres at the base to 800 metres.

Donnelly's Weir

Donnelly's Creek is named after Julia and Michael Donnelly, who were granted land selection near the junction of the Watts River and Donnelly's Creek in the 1870s. In 1893, Donnelly's Creek was diverted to augment the Maroondah Aqueduct. A picnic ground was established and trees planted, and by the early 1900s Donnelly's Weir was a popular beauty spot.

Meyers Creek Falls

A tramway following Meyers Creek to Crowley's Mill was very popular with tourists since the early 1900s. They travelled on timber trams to the falls for sightseeing and picnics. Meyers Creek Falls are rarely visited now as they are not easily accessed from Meyers Creek Road.

The Big Bouquet

The Big Bouquet is a flower farm and alpaca stud. Its gerbera farm is housed in a 12,000-square-metre Dutch glasshouse that holds 62,000 plants. A revolutionary hydroponic system has proved so efficient that the majority of gerbera growers now utilise the system. Visitors can learn about the growing of gerberas and breeding of alpacas, and enjoy a delicious lunch or Devonshire tea in the coffee shop.

Queens Park

Queens Park, near the centre of Healesville, is a popular place for picnics. It has free electric barbecues, a covered eating area, outdoor picnic tables and an excellent playground. The park also has tennis courts, a skate park and a delightful rose garden. In 1901, a picnic attended by 4000 people was held here.

Giant Steps / Innocent Bystander

This single winery has two distinct wines. Giant Steps focuses on the distinctive expression of single vineyard sites in the Yarra Valley, so each wine is a faithful expression of vintage and culture. Innocent Bystander sources fruit from great vineyards, creating wines with abundant fruit flavours.

A bistro provides food to match the wine, featuring wood-fired pizza, artisan bakery, cheese room, provedore and roasted coffee beans.

Hedgend Maze

Hedgend Maze has eight hectares of activities for all ages. Attractions include Australian Mural Eye Spy, Giant Chess and Checkers, Frisbee Golf, Laser Strike, and an 18-hole mini-golf course.

There are three mazes. The Hedge Maze has over 1200 metres of pathway. The path through the maze changes, so there is always a challenge. The Pavement Maze is a serious challenge, with a prize for solving the puzzle. There is also a four-colour Rainbow Maze.

Long Gully Estate

Long Gully Estate aims to produce the best possible, distinctive, cool-climate Yarra Valley wines at competitive prices. The wines have worldwide recognition, garnering nine trophies and over 300 medals at major shows. Long Gully Estate is one of the larger 'boutique' vineyards, with 22 hectares.

The Long Gully motto is 'Life is too short to drink bad wine!'

Magic Garden Roses

Magic Garden Roses offers the best garden roses in Australia, showcased within a spectacular and fragrant rose garden. Over 600 varieties of roses and over 100,000 rose plants grow on the property. These include bare-rooted and potted rosebushes, standard roses, carpet roses, David Austin Roses, climbing roses, old-world roses, modern shrub roses, mini roses, thornless roses and weeping roses.

The Healesville Labyrinth Garden

The Healesville Community Labyrinth is a project by Eastern Access Community Health (EACH) and the Yarra Ranges Council. The garden was designed by international landscape architect Jon Coe and features a seven-circuit classic labyrinth created in porphyry stone and Castlemaine slate.

The Grape Arbour is constructed from recycled railway lines and features a poem by Kath Holten in remembrance of the 2009 bushfires. Mosaic tiles were painted by over 300 community members as their contribution to the project.

Mt Rael

Mt Rael is famous for its spectacular views across the Yarra Valley. It is positioned high on four hectares, with 180-degree views. The local restaurant has an excellent seasonal menu sourced from local produce. There are five luxury suites and a sculpture garden available.

What sunshine is to flowers, smiles are to humanity. These are but trifles, to be sure; but scattered along life's pathway, the good they do is inconceivable.

Joseph Addison (1672–1719)

RiverStone Estate

RiverStone Estate produces premium quality wines for the domestic and international markets. The RiverStone Estate homestead and cellar door are built from bluestone and 100-year-old timber.

The homestead operates as a bed-and-breakfast, so it is possible to enjoy wine, food, entertainment, stunning views of the Yarra Valley and stay overnight.

The Slow Coach Dining Carriage

Victoria's only horse-drawn restaurant

Strathvea Guesthouse

Strathvea Guesthouse is an authentic traditional -style guesthouse. The heritage-listed 1920s house is an idyllic mountain hideaway set on two hectares of English-style garden surrounded by towering rainforest. Strathvea's garden has vibrant rhododendrons, camellias, azaleas, Pink Dogwoods and clouds of cherry and apple blossom. Oaks, Copper Beeches, Golden Elms, Japanese Maples, chestnuts and tulip trees display their colours in autumn.

Strathvea is one of the last historic guesthouses in Healesville.

The guesthouse has a large, shady verandah, three sitting rooms, open fires and a traditional dining room. It is able to accommodate 22 adults.

Yarra Valley Railway

In 1888, the Lilydale line was extended to Yarra Flats, with stations at Coldstream and Yering. There was a long trestle bridge that crossed the Yarra River and was part of the three kilometres of bridges beween Lilydale and Healesville. The line was exended through Tarrawarra to Healesville in 1889.

In 1901, the Duke and Duchess of York travelled to Healesville by train on their Victorian tour. The railway transformed Healesville into a tourist destination, with three trains running daily to Healesville in 1893. Timber, livestock, milk and dairy products were also transported.

Diesel rail cars replaced those run by steam for the passenger service in 1957, and the line was officially closed in 1983 due to a decline in track conditions and passenger numbers. Track restoration is now in progress. Train rides take passengers 4.5 kilometres to the far side of Tunnel Hill and is set to take passengers to Train Trak winery and Yarra Glen.

W250 is a W-class Diesel-Hydraulic Locomotive.

RM22

The railway runs train rides on RM22 from Healesville to Tunnel Hill, crossing the Watts River, under the Donovan's Road overbridge and through the historic tunnel. RM22 is a 153-horsepower Walker railmotor built in 1948.

This brick-lined historic tunnel is 154 metres long and was constructed in 1888.

The coal-burning steam locomotive J516 is under restoration.

Badger Creek

Badger Creek adjoins the picturesque township of Healesville and was part of the village settlement scheme. Unemployment in Melbourne was very high in 1893, and the government set up village settlements outside Melbourne to ease this situation. Badger Creek was surveyed as a township in 1894. Its post office opened around 1902 and closed in 1930. The creek was named after the wombats in the area, which were often called badgers.

Badger Creek School

View over the vineyard to Mount Riddell

Nolan Vineyard

Nolan Vineyard has two hectares of select Pinot Noir grape varieties, complemented with a Sauvignon Blanc planting. The site is on an ancient creek bed in the valley floor, producing wines with intense aromas and flavours with varietal characters.

Since 2004, Nolan Vineyard has produced vintages of Pinot Noir and Pinot Rose. Owners Myrtle and John Nolan are passionate about their wines and sharing the winery experience.

Badger Creek Blueberry Farm, Winery & Café

Located close to the Healesville Sanctuary is the Blueberry Farm, Winery & Café. Fresh berries are available from December to February, and frozen berries all year round. The café specialises in home-cooked morning and afternoon teas. A range of fruit wines is available, including a unique blueberry sparkling wine.

Badger Weir Park

Badger Creek has supplied Melbourne with water since 1908. The first weir redirected water from the creek to the Maroondah scheme. This was replaced in 1929 with a new weir, which supplies up to 110 megalitres of water a day to the Silvan Reservoir. There are several short walking trails through fern gullies and forest. The one-kilometre walk to Badger Weir follows the course of the open-channel aqueduct.

The Superb Lyrebird, Crimson Rosella and Australian King Parrot live in the forest of Mountain Ash (*Eucalyptus regnans*), Messmate (*Eucalyptus obliqua*) and Manna Gum (*Eucalyptus viminalis*).

The park has attracted visitors since the early 1900s. There is a popular picnic area and walking tracks through the fern gullies.

Australian King Parrot (*Alisterus scapularis*)

Badger Weir was also known as Coranderrk Weir, named after the Coranderrk Aboriginal Station.

Healesville Sanctuary

The sanctuary has a program to save the Helmeted Honeyeater, Tasmanian Devil and other endangered animals. Dr Colin MacKenzie leased land and set up the Institute of Anatomical Research in 1921 to study native animals for medical research. He moved to Canberra and entrusted the land to the Healesville Council in 1927. It opened as the Sir Colin MacKenzie Sanctuary for Australian Flora and Fauna in 1934, and today it is known as the Healesville Sanctuary.

Koala (*Phascolarctos cinereus*)

Echidna (*Tachyglossus aculeatus*)

The echidna eats ants and termites with its sticky, long tongue and curls up into a ball or burrows itself into the ground when it feels threatened. It lays one egg in its pouch, and when the puggle (baby echidna) starts to grow spines, the mother moves the baby out of the pouch into a burrow.

Common Wombat (*Vombatus ursinus*)

Wombats are solitary animals and weigh up to 40 kilograms. Their burrows can be 20 metres long, with many chambers. They leave the burrow at night to eat grass and have excellent hearing and smell.

Emu (*Dromaius novaehollandiae*)

Emus are one of the largest birds in the world. They can travel great distances and run up to 50 kilometres an hour. Emus swallow stones to help grind up food. They can also swim and like to play in water.

Laughing Kookaburra (*Dacelo novaeguineae*)

Dingo (*Canis lupus dingo*)

Red Kangaroo (*Macropus rufus*)

Australian Pelican (*Pelecanus conspicillatus*)

Barn Owl (*Tyto alba*)

Tasmanian Devil (*Sarcophilus harrisii*)

Tasmanian Devils have powerful jaws and teeth, which enable them to eat fur and bones as well as carcasses. The Devils' spine-chilling howls and savage behaviour suits its fearful name. Their natural habitat is restricted to the Tasmanian forests and countryside. The Healesville Sanctuary has a breeding program to save the Devils from extinction, particularly as a result of the Devil Facial Tumour Disease.

Superb Lyrebird (*Menura novaehollandiae*)

The male lyrebird performs an elaborate dance of courtship on a mound, using an amazing repertoire of imitated bird songs and sounds for his partner.

Lace Monitor / Tree Goanna (*Varanus varius*)

Lace Monitors can grow up to two metres in length. They are one of Australia's largest carnivorous lizards. They have strong claws, a long, forked tongue, and scale trees very quickly. They are related to the Perentie, Australia's largest lizard, and Indonesia's Komodo Dragon.

Spirits of the Sky

The 'Birds of Prey' show is world-famous.

Platypus (*Ornithorhynchus anatinus*)

Platypus are difficult to keep in captivity because of their voracious appetite. The first platypus to be bred in captivity, named Corrie, was hatched at the sanctuary in the 1940s. The platypus has fur, a duck-like bill, webbed feet and a tail like a beaver's. The males have a venomous spur, while the females lay eggs and feed their young milk.

Coranderrk Bushland Reserve

The Healesville Sanctuary is custodian of land that was once part of the Coranderrk Aboriginal Reserve. Coranderrk is the native name for Christmas Bush (*Prostanthera lasianthos*), a beautiful white flowering summer plant indigenous to the area. In 1863, 930 hectares of land was selected to establish Coranderrk Station, which was closed in 1924. In 1920, Sir Colin MacKenzie leased 31 hectares from the Aboriginal Protection Board to work with Australian fauna. This was the catalyst for the creation of the Healesville Sanctuary.

Lake Coranderrk

The 142-hectare Coranderrk Bushland Reserve is the largest remnant of intact Yarra Valley floor forest. The reserve is home to 10 percent of Victoria's plant species, 196 species of birds, 42 species of mammals, and 37 species of reptiles, frogs and fish.

Scarred Tree

The bark was removed from this tree to make a canoe.

Superintendent's Residence

This two-storey house was built in 1883 as the residence of the superintendent at the Coranderrk Aboriginal Station.

William Barak

Barak: last chief of the Yarra Yarra Tribe of Aborigines by Florence Ada Fuller (1867–1946), 1885
Pictures Collection, State Library of Victoria

Barak was a skilled artist. His paintings and artifacts are highly valued and are held in museums around the world. He painted in ochre and charcoal, as well as the European mediums of gouache and watercolour. His art is a powerful record of his culture.

William Barak (1818–1903) was an outstanding leader and great Australian. He was born in Brushy Creek and was the last leader of the Yarra Yarra tribe. Barak witnessed the signing of the 'treaty' between John Batman (1801–1839) and Indigenous tribal elders in 1835. He received education from 1837 to 1839 at Reverend Langhorne's Mission House, located at the site of the Shrine of Remembrance.

Originally named 'Beruk', he was given the name William, along with the European pronunciation of his name, upon joining the Native Police Corps.

Barak was a mounted trooper with the Native Police Corps from 1844 to 1851, serving as a tracker for Captain Henry Dana.

After he left the police, Barak lived with his friends the de Purys on their estate at Yeringberg, and also at John and Ann Bon's Wappan Station, now submerged by Eildon Dam. He settled at Acheron in 1859 with his first wife, Lizzie, hoping to have the area reserved.

In 1963, Barak moved to Coranderrk Station, which became a successful Aboriginal farming community. Homes were built and land cleared for wheat crops, vegetables and cattle. Coranderrk included a school, dairy, church, store, butchery, bakery, brick and hop kilns, and orphan dormitories. It supplied produce, milk and bread to the communities in Lilydale and Healesville.

Having lived before the arrival of the Europeans, Barak saw the displacement and death of his people, whom he tried to help. He liaised between officials and the native population, working tirelessly to protect the rights and culture of his people. He was highly respected, both among the Indigenous people and the European settlers, even becoming known as 'King Barak'.

Barak married three times and was the father of three children, all of whom he outlived.

Barak is buried in Coranderrk Cemetery along with 300 members of the Yarra Yarra tribe.

HODDLES CREEK

Hoddles Creek is named after surveyor Robert Hoddle, who led the first European expedition to find the source of the Yarra River in 1844.

Hoddles Creek was one of the longest-lasting goldfields in the Upper Yarra area. Gold was discovered here around 1859, and Hoddles Creek gold was reputedly the purest in Victoria. The gold-bearing leads followed the main creek, which were worked over by thousands of prospectors. The lower diggings at the junction of Gembrook and Parkinsons roads were a major mining site. At this location, a settlement grew, and by 1862 it had a post office and store.

World-famous scientist, Professor Harrie Massey (1908–1983), was born in and had a great love for Hoddles Creek. The local school has a plaque in his honour.

The Big Berry

The Big Berry produces premium Yarra Valley raspberries, blueberries and blackberries. The farm was established in 1985 on 16 hectares of rich red soil. The temperate climate and fertile soil are perfect for growing a variety of berries.

On the motionless branches of some trees, autumn berries hung like clusters of coral beads, as in those fabled orchards where the fruits were jewels.

Charles Dickens (1812–1870)

Robert Hoddle

Robert Hoddle, painted by his granddaughter Agnes Grant McDonald, c. 1885–90
Pictures Collection, State Library of Victoria

Robert Hoddle (1794–1881) was born in Westminster, London. He was accepted as a cadet in the Corps of Royal Military Surveyors and Draftsmen at 15 years of age. Hoddle arrived in New South Wales in 1823, where he was appointed assistant surveyor.

Hoddle arrived at Port Phillip in 1837, and was appointed senior surveyor, designing the layout of Melbourne, Williamstown and Geelong in 1838 and many country areas of Victoria. He was also an accomplished artist.

Before 1836, little was known of Victoria's geography. The surveyors were able to map the positions of mountain ranges and peaks, lakes and major rivers, and design over 100 settlements. Hoddle was appointed Victoria's first Surveyor General in 1851.

The Hoddle family lived in a fine house built in 1842 on the corner of Bourke and Spencer streets. He spent his years of retirement tending the garden and enjoying his collection of books and pictures.

Robert Hoddle Dec. 1845 near Source of Yarra Yarra River Starvation Creek by Henry Short (1807–1865), 1860
Pictures Collection, State Library of Victoria

KINGLAKE

Gold was discovered on Mount Slide in 1861 at an area known as Mountain Rush. The Mountain Rush post office opened in 1862, but closed in 1863 as the miners moved to other locations and timber cutting replaced mining.

Kinglake township was later established at the top of the Great Dividing Range. It was named after British historian and surveyor Alexander William Kinglake, who in 1870 surveyed the route from Queenstown to Glenburn. Kinglake's post office opened in 1883. By the 1920s, the timber supply was running out and potato and berry farming became the main industries.

House of Bottles

This unusual building, constructed between 1969 and 1972, was made from 13,569 bottles. The nearby Dutch windmill was built with 5000 bottles.

Bollygum Park

This unique park is based on the children's book *Bollygum* by Australian author Garry Fleming. The park tells a bush story to educate visitors about native animal habitats and Indigenous culture. Bollygum Park includes Wombat House, Frogmouth House and Platypus House.

Lady Stonehaven's Lookout

John Baird, 1st Viscount Stonehaven, GCMG, DSO, PC, JP, DL (1874–1941), served as the eighth governor-general of Australia. His wife, Lady Stonehaven (1874–1974), was the daughter of the 10th Earl of Kintore. The Melbourne Central Business District can be seen from this lookout.

Jehoshaphat Gully

King Jehoshaphat is a Biblical person who plundered gold from his defeated enemies after they fled without fighting. Gold miners named this area during the gold rush of 1861. In 1928, Kinglake National Park was established due to the efforts of Sir James Barrett (1862–1945), a worker for Victoria's National Parks; William Everard (1869–1950), a local politician; and Professor William Laver (1866–1940), who donated 22 hectares of his land at Jehoshaphat Gully.

Above all, do not lose your desire to walk. Every day I walk myself into a state of well-being and walk away from every illness. I have walked myself into my best thoughts and I know of no thought so burdensome that one cannot walk away from it … if one just keeps on walking, everything will be alright.

Søren Kierkegaard (1813–1855)

Wombelano Falls

Wombelano is an Indigenous word meaning 'very pretty' or 'beautiful'.

LAUNCHING PLACE

In the mid-1800s, bullock drays from Lilydale travelled only as far as Launching Place. Flat-bottomed punts were then launched into the river at Launching Place, carrying goods upstream. When the punts had travelled as far as possible, the supplies were carried by packhorse to the settlers and miners living scattered around the goldfields.

In 1861 the nearest railway was Hawthorn, and by 1882 the railway reached Lilydale. In 1887 it was decided that a road between Lilydale and Warburton would be built.

Home Hotel

John and Catherine Ewart arrived in Launching Place in the 1840s and here they set up a store, hotel and post office. The Home Hotel, first known as Ewarts, began as a large slab hut. The name Home Hotel originated in the 1860s and 1870s, when prospectors would come for a meal after weeks of hardship in the hills. The early hotel had a huge fireplace at one end, offering the comfort of home. In 1891, the famous French actress Sarah Bernhardt and her entourage enjoyed a two-day stay at the hotel.

Yarra Valley Archery Park

The park offers indoor and outdoor archery ranges, undercover golf driving practice, a pool table and chess. A light meal or coffee can also be enjoyed at the café.

Haining Farm

Haining Farm is one of the few remaining dairy farms in the Yarra Valley. Comprising 65 hectares, it started around 1925 and was donated to the State Government in 1974. The farm is now managed by Parks Victoria.

In addition to operating as a commercial dairy, the farm is an educational resource for thousands of school children visiting each year.

Its name hails from a property in Linlithgow Shire, Scotland.

> *I had rather be on my farm than be emperor of the world.*
>
> George Washington (1732–1799)

The Don River meanders through the property.

Rotary Dairy

The dairy milks 110 to 150 Jersey and Friesian cows. In the farm's early history, milking finished at 7.30 am, with a rush to transport the milk cans by horse and cart to Launching Place station to meet the 8.00 am train to Melbourne.

Wanderslore Sanctuary

Prospecting for gold occurred here in the late 1800s and also in the Depression of the 1930s. Artist, poet and teacher Constance Coleman (1903–1990) inherited a fishing shack on a small block of land in 1932. Constance devoted her income to acquiring adjoining bush blocks to create a nine-hectare bushland sanctuary.

Wanderslore is named after the magic garden in Walter de la Mare's *Memoirs of a Midget*. It contains three main types of vegetation: dry sclerophyll, damp sclerophyll and riparian forests. Fungi, native grasses and orchids are plentiful at the sanctuary, which is also home to 13 indigenous ferns species and 90 species of birds. Other creatures found at Wanderslore are wallabies, wombats, echidnas, antechinuses, possums, bandicoots and goannas.

The sanctuary has an annual open day.

The Studio

Constance painted in watercolour and oil in her studio, which was previously the office at Launching Place railway station.

LILYDALE

Billanook was the name given by the local Wurundjeri people to the site that became the Lillydale (later, Lilydale) township. Squatters on large pastoral runs were the first Europeans to settle in the Lilydale area. Land was sold in the township in 1860, and by 1862 a post office, blacksmith's shop and store were established. In the 1870s, churches and a school were built and the town had become the centre for livestock sales. The railway line was extended to Lilydale in 1881, stimulating growth by transporting produce to Melbourne's markets and bringing tourists who stayed at guesthouses in the area.

David Mitchell, a stonemason from Scotland, arrived in Australia in 1852. He was the father of famous Australian operatic soprano Dame Nellie Melba, who is buried in the Lilydale Cemetery. He employed many of Lilydale's population.

Lilydale was possibly named by surveyor John Hardy after a song of the period called 'Lilly Dale' or in honour of Lilly de Castella, the wife of Swiss pioneer Paul de Castella. The spelling later changed to that of the flower.

Lilydale Court House

The Lilydale Court House, built in 1876, is now home to the Lilydale and District Historical Society.

Anglican Church of St John the Baptist

The church was built around 1872. Prince Charles attended the church when he visited Australia.

Queen Victoria Jubilee Avenue

The trees on Main Street from Cave Hill Road to the railway crossing commemorate the 50th anniversary of the reign of Queen Victoria in 1897. Oak trees were planted by important citizens and named after them, celebrations were held and a public holiday, Arbor Day, was announced. Arbor Day remained an annual holiday until 1920.

Mechanics' Institute, Athenaeum and Free Library

The Athenaeum was built in 1888 for social activities and concerts. Dame Nellie Melba sang here on many occasions. Today it is the home of the Athenaeum Theatre Company, and a museum contained in the building houses Dame Nellie Melba memorabilia. Lilydale's old Shire Offices and Council Chambers, located on the left of the Athenaeum, were built in 1889.

Cooring Yering

David Mitchell built this vineyard and homestead in 1884 for Colonel G. Hutton, the founder of Smallgoods. It is one of the largest mansions built in the district, containing 35 rooms.

The Towers

Alfred Hand, a tanner and viticulturist, inherited seven hectares from his father, Richard Hand, in 1871 and built a home there in 1876. Andrew and Elizabeth Fulton, the next owners, built the second stage including twin towers with castellations. In 1893, Edward Janson purchased the property and named it The Towers. He used the name on his famous wine and included an image of the estate on the label.

Lillydale Lake

Cashin's Flour Mill

Cashin's Flour Mill operated from the early 1850s, crushing wheat grown in the Lilydale district. Mr Hugh Kneen from Port Arlington built the mill for James Cashin and his family, whose cottage overlooked the mill.

A timber waterwheel on the side of the mill was driven by water along an aqueduct, filled from a weir on Olinda Creek. The mill closed in 1876 because of failed crops in the area. Two stone walls near the lake are the only reminders of Cashin's Flour Mill.

Yarra Valley Herb Farm

The Yarry Valley Herb Farm includes a restaurant and the Redgum Australia Gallery. A wide variety of fresh and dried herbs are available to purchase.

Melba Park

Established in the 1860s on land surrounding the Athenaeum, old Shire Offices and Council Chambers, the reserve was renamed Melba Park in honour of Dame Nellie Melba.

The Mafeking Tree

Located at the edge of Melba Park, the tree was planted by the people of Lilydale in 1900. It was planted to commemorate the gallant and successful defence of Mafeking, South Africa, by Colonel Baden-Powell and his brave garrison during a siege by the Boers over a period of 209 days.

Bianchet Winery and Bistro

Originally a market garden, vines were planted by Lou and Theresa Bianchet in 1976. Grape varieties grown include Merlot, Cabernet Sauvignon, Cabernet Franc, Shiraz, Malbec, Pinot Noir, Chardonnay, Traminer and Verduzzo. Bianchet is one of only a few vineyards in Australia that grow Verduzzo, and commercially producing a full-bodied and full-flavoured Verduzzo wine.

Providence Ponds
– Private Garden

Merilyn and Peter Wheatfill bought the 0.2-hectare property in the year 2000. They built a beautiful garden that includes seven ponds, Canadian Maples, a Canary Island Date Palm, Chinese Paulownias, a Horse Chestnut, a heritage-listed Golden Elm, and 185 roses.

MARYSVILLE

Paradise Plains was an area in dense forest that was first settled in the early 1860s. John Steavenson, Assistant Commissioner for Roads and Bridges, made Marysville his headquarters while overseeing the construction of roads to the goldfields. The Yarra Track was re-routed over Robley's Spur and the Cumberland in 1863, which proved an easier track to the goldfields. Steavenson surveyed the town site around 1863 and named it after his wife Mary Martha Murphy. The settlement at Paradise Plains was then abandoned in favour of Marysville in 1864. After the decline of gold prospecting in 1914, the era of tourism commenced. Marysville became known as Melbourne's honeymoon capital, with visitors attracted by bushwalks and Steavenson Falls. Coaches took tourists to accommodation houses at Marysville and Alexandra, via the popular Black Spur. Marysville is an ideal destination for bushwalking and getting back to nature.

Street Trees

The street trees in Marysville were planted by school-children in 1890. They are now mature Oak trees which line Murchison Street.

The Camp

The first tents for the village of Marysville were pitched by the river around 1863.

Beauty Spot Nature Trail

The trail among the tree ferns follows Leary's Creek and is suitable for people with limited mobility.

Gould Memorial Drive

The Gould Memorial Drive with its two rows of Lombardy Poplars
provides a picturesque roadway into Marysville from Buxton. The trees
commemorate the lives of Joy and Lloyd Gould, early pioneers of Marysville.

The Big Culvert

The Big Culvert is a bluestone arch culvert on the historic Yarra Track near Cambarville. The beautiful moss-covered arch was one of five constructed by German settler and stonemason George Koehler in the 1860s.

A highlight of the area is the display of ferns and trees in the rainforest gully.

Bruno's Art & Sculpture Garden

The original and unique artworks of sculptor and painter Bruno Torfs bring joy and inspiration to visitors from all over the world. Nestled among the luscious rainforest setting is a collection of over 150 characters lovingly handcrafted by Bruno. It is a world rich in fantasy and beauty inspired by his journeys to some of the world's most intriguing and remote regions. On the property is a gallery displaying over 200 of his artworks, including oil paintings, sketches and smaller sculptures.

Imagination is more important than knowledge.

Albert Einstein (1879–1955)

Cambarville

During the 1860s, Cambarville was an important stopping point along the Yarra Track to the Woods Point goldfields. Later, Cambarville became a timber town with a steam-driven sawmill, houses, school and shops. Near Cambarville is the Cumberland Memorial Scenic Reserve, notable for its giant Mountain Ash trees.

Golden Bower Water Race

The 16-kilometre-long water race was built by gold miners in 1913 to channel water to the Sovereign and Golden Bower mines near the Reefton Spur. It later supplied water to the Cumberland Falls goldmine (originally Kirwans Reward) and to the Anderson & Sons Big River Saw Milling Company.

Sitka Spruce

This spruce tree was planted in the late 1930s by forest ranger Jack Lewis to mark the site of the house of 'The Hermit of Cumberland', George Loch (1860–1941). Loch was a gold prospector and timber cutter who established the clearing and lived in a timber cabin.

Avenue of Ferns

The avenue marks the route of the Yarra Track, used by thousands of miners in the 1860s. Ferns were cut and placed over boggy sections of the track and have grown to produce the avenue of closely-spaced tree ferns.

Cambarville Historic Township

The two tree stumps border the main street of the once-thriving town.

Cumberland Falls

Cumberland Falls takes its name from Cumberland Creek. Viewing access to the falls is difficult due to steep terrain.

The Big Tree

A huge Mountain Ash known as The Big Tree was once one of the tallest trees in Victoria. It has a girth of 5.2 metres and is 84 metres tall (wind damage in 1959 had reduced its height from 92 metres). In the 1930s, 1000 people visited the reserve each weekend.

Cora Lyn Falls

Lady Talbot Drive

Lady Talbot Drive is named after the wife of Sir Reginald Talbot (1841–1929), Governor of Victoria from 1904 to 1908. Lady Talbot (1855–1937) was president of the Talbot Colony for Epileptics and promoted social welfare.

Near the start of Lady Talbot Drive is Michaeldene Track, which follows the Taggerty River and includes a trestle bridge, timber tramway, The Wishing Well and the Island Hop.

The Wishing Well

The Wishing Well is a natural spring.

Keppel Falls Lookout

The magnificence of Keppel Falls can be seen in their entirety from the lookout.

LEFT
Lady Talbot Drive is a 48-kilometre road loop. The first 11 kilometres follow the Taggerty River, past picnic areas and Phantom Falls.

The Island Hop

The Island Hop consists of a circuit of bridges across a number of islands.

Phantom Falls

Phantom Falls is a short, steep walk from the Taggerty River to a fern gully where Phantom Falls Creek weaves its way. The falls are thought to have been named by Jeremiah Keppel, who settled in the area in the 1880s. Like a phantom, Keppel observed, the falls appear out of nowhere.

Meeting of the Waters

The Taggerty River and Whitehouse Creek merge at the 'Meeting of the Waters'.

The Beeches

The Beeches is a unique stand of old Myrtle Beech trees.

Lake Mountain

Lake Mountain is the second-closest place to Melbourne (after Mount Donna Buang) where visitors can enjoy snow, with a popular cross-country ski resort there. The mountain rises to 1420 metres above sea level, with seven toboggan runs and two main ski runs. Lake Mountain was named after George Lake, who was the Surveyor General of the area.

The Snow Gum (*Eucalyptus pauciflora*) woodland

ABOVE
There are over 40 kilometres of ski trails and walking tracks on Lake Mountain. Panoramic views, along with wild flowers in spring and summer, can be enjoyed from lookouts.

During winter, Lake Mountain is popular with cross-country skiers and tobogganists.

In 1864, Maurice and Francis Keppel purchased land at Paradise Plains on Edgar's Track, which was used by packhorses between Warburton and Woods Point. The Keppels also bought land at Buxton and around Lake Mountain, moving cattle and sheep between their pastures.

The last cattle grazed on Lake Mountain in 1964. Keppel's surviving descendant presented the Lands Department one of the longest-held grazing licences in Victoria's history.

The Public Works Department initiated the development of the Lake Mountain area in the early 1920s, with the construction of a road. The Ski Club of Victoria visited Lake Mountain in the late 1930s, but it was not until 1939 that the area was open for skiing.

Lake Mountain is a popular destination throughout the year. In summer there are over 40 kilometres of cross-country ski trails to explore on foot or bike, flying foxes, dune buggies, laser skirmish, disc golf, a jumping castle and tube runs.

Keppell's Hut

The hut was built in 1939 by Maurice and Francis Keppel. It has been rebuilt after being destroyed by fire in 1983 and 2009. Keppel's Hut is a popular destination for horseriders and skiers during winter.

Lake Mountain Visitor Centre

Steavenson Falls

Steavenson Falls takes its name from the Steavenson
River, which was named by surveyor John Steavenson
who visited the area in 1862. A track to the falls was
cut in 1866 to attract tourists.

Steavenson Falls is one of Victoria's highest
waterfalls, cascading 84 metres over three levels into
the Steavenson River valley.

Trout and Salmon Ponds

Nestled on the slopes of Mount Gordon, the Marysville Trout and Salmon Ponds was first developed in the early 1980s.

The ponds are fed by water flowing from the surrounding mountains. This water is pure and crystal-clear, with no farm runoff and no human or chemical contamination.

It is a natural ecosystem and habitat for the fish, with reedy banks, overhanging trees and gently flowing waterfalls surrounded by tall peppermint, Stringybark and Messmate Eucalypts, Silverwood and Blackwood Wattles, native grasses and ferns. The fishing ponds are stocked with Rainbow Trout and Atlantic Salmon, ranging in size from 500 grams to 6 kilograms.

MILLGROVE

Millgrove takes its name from the property of early land selector John Kennedy on the north side of the Yarra River, named after his hometown in Tipperary County, Ireland. Millgrove received timber from the Dee River valley, under the peaks of Ben Cairn, Donna Buang and Little Joe. Its post office opened in 1906 and the area is based on timber milling and agriculture.

In 1945, Tom Inverarity and his brother-in-law, Charlie 'Boxer' Baird, established a mill at Millgrove.

Bowerbird Salvaged Timbers owns the sawmill and specialises in uniquely designed, finely crafted furniture, kitchens and joinery services. They use ethically collected, kiln-dried, solid timbers.

O'Shannassy Aqueduct Trail

In 1910 the O'Shannassy Catchment was set aside to supply water to Melbourne. The scheme to harvest water from the O'Shannassy River commenced in 1911, and in 1914 the 78-kilometre-long, open concrete aqueduct and pipeline was completed. The gravity-fed channel delivered 90 million litres a day. With the growing use of the Yarra–Silvan pipelines in the 1950s and the Yarra Valley pipeline in the 1970s, the need for the O'Shannassy aqueduct diminished. It was decommissioned in 1997 and was bestowed to the State Government for inclusion into the Yarra Ranges National Park in 2005. Today, it offers one of the most outstanding walking experiences within Victoria.

Dee Split Bridge

Constructed from local Mountain Ash timber in 1947, Dee Slip Bridge is a reminder of a land slip disaster. The O'Shannassy aqueduct was damaged by the land slip, requiring the channel to be reinforced with a steel flume. It is the only trestle bridge on the O'Shannassy aqueduct trail.

Giant tree ferns can be found in the bush around Millgrove.

Platts Falls

The falls were a popular attraction for visitors to Millgrove in the early 1900s. A tramway followed Frenchman's Creek to where the Platts brothers operated a sawmill. It was also possible to reach the falls via a walking track from Ben Cairn. Since the 1940s, access into the catchment area has beem restricted. However, with the decommissioning of the O'Shannassy aqueduct in 1997, it is possible to once again see this beautiful waterfall, even though it is located in untracked forest.

NOOJEE

A picturesque Gippsland town, *Noojee* is named after the Aboriginal word meaning 'valley of' or 'place of rest'. Gold prospectors and tin miners settled in the area in the mid-1860s, later followed by farmers and timber workers. Noojee was once a major timber town, using the railway to Warragul to transport timber, freight and passengers.

A river seems a magic thing. A magic, moving, living part of the very earth itself — for it is from the soil, both from its depth and from its surface, that a river has its beginning.

Laura Gilpin (1891–1979)

Possibly the most famous of the many prospectors of the area was the eccentric Englishman Dick Belpoole. Belpoole was unsatisfied with the durability of clothing and built a tin suit to wear in the bush, which helped him travel through blackberries and thick undergrowth. He found a rich gold deposit and carried large amounts of gold to Noojee. The location of Dick's 'Mother Lode' was never disclosed.

Noojee Trestle Bridge

Known as Number 7, this is the only remaining of seven trestle bridges on the section of railway line between Nayook and Noojee. It is 102 metres long and 20 metres high. The line was opened in sections from 1890 to 1919 and rebuilt after bushfires destroyed it in 1939. The bridge was taken out of service when the line was closed in 1954.

Toorongo Falls

The Little Toorongo River is fed by a stream from the Toorongo Plateau, which never dries up.

Amphitheatre Falls

Surrounded by green ferns and located on the Toorongo River is Amphitheatre Falls.

Tall Timbers – Private Garden

Olwyn and Manfred Scharley created a garden that offers shaded walks among azaleas, ferns, maples and rhododendrons, a landscaped creek with cascades, and a series of lakes and ponds. Exotic plants are merged with the surrounding forest.

The award-winning garden is named after the tall timber surrounding the property.

POWELLTOWN

Powelltown, located in the Yarra State Park, began as a sawmilling town. It was known as Blake's or Blake's Mills until 1912, when it was renamed Powelltown. The town was named after the Victorian Powell Wood Process Company, which developed the 'Powell' method of using water, arsenic and molasses to preserve timber.

Surrounded by magnificent Mountain Ash, Myrtle Beech and Messmate Stringybark, ferns and damp gullies, Powelltown operated one of the biggest timber mills in the area.

A system of tram tracks opened up the area in the early 1900s and logs were transported to the sawmills. The Upper Yarra Valley forest area in the 1920s included over 200 timber mills — then the largest timber producer in Victoria.

There are a number of old tramline walks where remnants of the timber milling era can be found. The huge logs on the log bogies and the winch give an idea of the large scale of the timber industry.

The original timber cottages, built in 1912, once belonged to the largest timber mill in Victoria called the Victorian Powell Wood Process Company.

Ada Tree Scenic Reserve

The Ada Tree, a giant Mountain Ash (*Eucalyptus regnans*) approximately 300–400 years old, is one of the largest trees in Australia. It has a girth of 15.7 metres at chest height and a weight of approximately 225 tonnes. Its height is estimated to have been over 120 metres before the tree lost its upper branches to a storm in 1946. The tree now has a height of around 76 metres, with a root system of more than 0.2 hectares. The cool rainforest area is watered by the Little Ada River. The tree is protected in the Ada Tree Scenic Reserve.

The earth has music for those who will listen.

William Shakespeare (1564–1616)

Big Rock is located on Brahams Road en route to the Ada Tree.

Black Sands Road leads past groves of Myrtle Beech trees to an overgrown World War II airstrip and also to Mount Myrtalia, near where large numbers of tree ferns can be viewed.

Prospectors Werner and Joseph Marschalek discovered the tree in 1986 while fossicking for gold and gemstones. Werner Marschalek and Ray Wright took five years and $30,000 to set up a track to the Ada Tree which was opened in 1997. The Ada Tree and Ada River are believed to be named after Ada Mortimore (née Hansen), who lived in the area and was acquainted with the surveyor.

The Island Creek Walk to the Ada Tree leads through rainforest gullies, past groves of ancient Myrtle Beech, sassafras, tree ferns and fallen giants of the forest.

Gilderoy Falls

The remains of a logging track lead to the rarely viewed cascades of Gilderoy Falls, named after the town of Gilderoy.

Seven Acre Rock

A short walk to Seven Acre Rock reveals picturesque views over the Bunyip State Park. On a clear day, the Western Port and Port Phillip bays can be seen. Seven Acre Rock, a granite outcrop, is located approximately ten kilometres from Powelltown.

Starlings Gap

A sawmill operated at Starlings Gap until 1912. Old relics from the sawmilling days can still be seen in the area. The trees were cut down with cross-cut saws and axes and winched onto the tramways. From 1913 steam locomotives transported the timber, and from the 1930s motor locomotives were used.

Steam winches were used to pull logs over steep inclines. Starlings Gap Picnic Ground

View near Starlings Gap before forest regrowth

PANTON'S GAP

Panton's Gap is located between the mountains Ben Cairn (1022 metres) and Toolebewong (750 metres) at an altitude of 542 metres above sea level. Panton's Gap receives its name from Joseph Anderson Panton's small mountain home, which stood above the head of the valley.

The view from the Warburton-to-Healesville road near Ben Cairn, with the Dandenong Ranges (left) across to Melbourne's city buildings.

Joseph Panton

Joseph Anderson Panton (1831–1913), was born at Knockiemill, Aberdeenshire, Scotland. He was educated at the Scottish Naval and Military Academy and at the University of Edinburgh, leaving without a degree. In 1851, Panton migrated to Sydney and moved to the Port Phillip District. He tried farming and gold prospecting, and was appointed Assistant Commissioner at Kangaroo Gully in 1852, Senior Assistant Commissioner at Bendigo in 1853 and Senior Commissioner in 1854. His administration was commended by the commission, which inquired into affairs at the diggings after Eureka.

In 1858, Panton travelled to Scotland and Paris to study art with Hubert de Castella. On his return, he was appointed Warden and Magistrate at the Jamieson-Woods Point and Anderson's Creek goldfields. Afterwards, he became Magistrate at Heidelberg, during which time he mapped the Yarra Valley. He moved to Melbourne as Senior Magistrate in 1874 and stayed there until 1907.

Panton was active in the Victorian Artists Association and the Victorian Academy of Art. He was also a fellow of the Royal Geographical Society in London, as well as Vice-President of the Royal Geographical Society of Australasia. He helped organise the Melbourne Exhibition of 1854 and was Commissioner of the Melbourne International Exhibition of 1880.

Panton owned vineyards near Bendigo, producing prize-winning wines. He took up leases in the outer districts of New South Wales and Western Australia and later moved to a lease in the Northern Territory. In 1860 he married Eleanor Margaret, daughter of Colonel John Fulton of the Bengal Native Infantry. In 1895, Panton declined the honour of knighthood but was appointed Companion of the Order of St Michael and St George. He was survived by two daughters, Amy and Alice.

Joseph Panton, painted by his daughter Alice Julie Panton (1863–1960)
Pictures Collection, State Library of Victoria

Ben Cairn

Located halfway between Healesville and Warburton, Ben Cairn overlooks the Don Valley. A huge granite rock on Mount Ben Cairn was originally known as Ewart's Rock, and a feasible track to Ewart's Rock from the Don Valley Road was found. The 'Ben Cairn Rock', as it became known, was opened to the public in 1910 at a ceremony attended by officials and residents from Healesville, Launching Place and Warburton.

A waterfall located between Panton's Gap and Ben Cairn

Malleson's Glen

In the late 1890s, a Melbourne solicitor named Malleson owned an estate near the Don River at the foothills of Ben Cairn. Tourists were welcomed and allowed access to beauty spots in the glen. Malleson planted holly hedges and ferns to create a place of beauty with bridges and paths for people to explore.

At Malleson's Glen, visitors dined in the open air at a fern gully known as the Lover's Walk. They could also walk up Malleson's Track to Malleson's Lookout.

Only spread a fern-frond over a man's head and worldly cares are cast out, and freedom and beauty and peace come in.

John Muir (1838–1914)

Don Falls

The glen was known as a beautiful fern gully on the Don River.

Myrtle Creek Road Bridge
This unusual, curved bridge was built in the early 1900s.

Mount Toole be wong

The Donna Buang Range includes the steep slopes of the mountains Ben Cairn (1022 metres), Boobyalla (1200 metres), Donna Buang (1232 metres), Toole be wong (750 metres) and Victoria (1100 metres). The earlier inhabitants of this area, the Yarra tribes, referred to these ranges as *Thuonnabe wong*, meaning 'the place of the mist'; or *Tool-e-youang*, 'the ribs or thorax of the mountain'. The original name appears to have been modified into its current spelling of Toolebewong.

The locality is home to the Moora Moora Co-operative Community, an alternative-lifestyle group established in the 1970s. They seek to live in harmony with nature, using only solar and wind-generated power.

Earth and sky, woods and fields, lakes and rivers, the mountain and the sea, are excellent schoolmasters, and teach some of us more than we can ever learn from books.

John Lubbock (1834–1913)

RUBICON

Rubicon is a small town on the Rubicon River. It was home to the Tuanarong people for thousands of years. Timber harvesting was historically the major industry of the region. Logging commenced near Rubicon in 1905, with the logs taken to the closest town, Alexandra, by horsedrawn wooden track trains. Logging companies operated there until 1953.

The Historic Area is the site of the first Victorian hydro-electric power scheme. The Rubicon scheme, completed in 1929, consists of four power stations, three small run-of-river dams, aqueducts and pipelines. During the 1930s, the scheme contributed about 20 percent of Victoria's electricity requirements. The total generating capacity of the scheme today is 13 megawatts.

The Rubicon forest is an important habitat for a number of threatened species. One is the endangered Leadbeater's Possum (*Gymnobelideus leadbeateri*), one of Victoria's faunal emblems, a small, nocturnal and arboreal marsupial that lives in the hollows of old trees. Rubicon River is inhabited by Barred Galaxias (*Galaxias fuscus*), one of Australia's most threatened native fish. The Superb Lyrebird (*Menura novaehollandiae*) and Gang-Gang Cockatoo (*Callocephalon fimbriatum*) are also found in the area.

Rubicon Falls

Incline for the Rubicon Power Station. The Rubicon 'A' power station has a pipeline with a 443-metre drop over its 1305-metre length.

Fifteen Thousand Foot Siphon Trestle Bridge

This trestle bridge is so named due to the length of the tramline. A two-foot gauge steel tramway was built between Rubicon Power Station and Rubicon Dam, with timber trestle bridges at Fifteen Thousand Foot Siphon, Royston Power Station, Beech Creek and Lubra Creek. The tramway remained in operation until the 1990s.

Snobs Creek Falls

Snobs Creek Falls offer spectacular views as they drop over 100 metres. In the early 1860s, Snobs Creek was known as Cataract Creek, but was later changed to Snobs after Black Brooks, a West Indian man who operated a bootmaker's shop close to the creek. *Snob* is an old English term used for 'bootmaker' or 'boot repairer'.

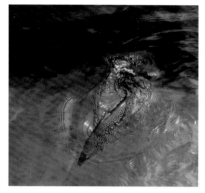

Snobs Creek Fish Hatchery

The hatchery is the largest in Victoria and breeds trout, Murray Cod, Golden Perch and salmon, releasing over one million fish each year. On display are magnificently preserved and live animals.

Mount Torbreck Summit Cairn

Mount Torbreck rises to an altitude of 1516 metres. The track to the summit commences at Barnewall Plains and rises 366 metres in elevation. The mountain has a drystone cairn erected by Thomas Wilkinson Pinniger (1837–1927) in 1866–67 at 3.2 metres high. Pinninger became Government Surveyor in 1852 and spent the next 20 years completing the geodetic survey of central Victoria. He designed the colony's first regional townships. His survey points are marked by large stone cairns, 17 of which have been located.

Seville

Seville was initially called 'a township in the parish of Wandin Yalloak' in 1885. It was later named Redlands, but as there was already a town with this name, it was renamed to Seville in 1886 after the daughter of resident William Smith, Miss Seville Smith. The town is located in the centre of a fruit-, berry- and vine-growing area.

Carriage Café Seville

Located on the Lilydale-to-Warburton Rail Trail, the Carriage Café is a four-minute walk from the old Seville Station. The 100-year-old carriage has air-conditioning and heating.

The Lilydale–Warburton trail follows the historical railway line to Warburton, which opened in 1901 and closed in 1964. The Rail Trail is popular with walkers, cyclists and horseriders.

War Memorial Park

Archimedes' Screw

Archimedes of Syracuse is believed to have invented the device in the third century BC. Turning the handle raises the water level.

Ainsworth Estate

Ainsworth Estate is a luxury accommodation facility and boutique winery. Its vineyard is magnificent all year round, and it has been described as the 'Jewel' of the Yarra Valley. The estate has won many awards, its vintages have won over 100 medals, and it has received accolades as a producer of fine, cool-climate wines. It has top-quality Shiraz, Pinot and Chardonnay and sparkling varieties.

Brumfield Winery

Brumfield Winery produces small batches of wine from a newly planted vineyard, providing an intimate tasting experience for visitors.

Anda's Kitchen offers relaxed, fresh food, prepared in-house. Alfresco dining can be enjoyed in the courtyard, indoor café or on a picnic rug under the huge palm tree.

The Art Space displays beautiful works of art.

Dalblair – Private Garden

Dalblair's bed-and-breakfast features three luxurious suites on 12 picturesque hectares. Started in 2004, its garden is filled with a range of bulbs, hellebores, gardenias, *Cyclamen*, *Campanula*, *Plectranthus*, *Tiarella*, *Thalictrum*, *Polygonatum multiflorum* and many others. The rose garden includes many species and rare types, such as a range of David Austin combined with Delbard roses, intermixed with species roses. Two vegetable plots also produce a range of vegetables each year.

Elmswood Estate

Elmswood Estate is a boutique winery with wines produced from vines ten to 30 years old. Seven varieties of grape are currently grown: Riesling, Sauvignon Blanc, Chardonnay, Pinot, Merlot, Cabernet Sauvignon and a small amount of Shiraz. The vines grow in rich red clay loam, which retains moisture extremely well.

Fine wines and weddings are the speciality of Elmswood Estate, with its combination of stunning photographic opportunities and the glassed room, The Pavilion, as the perfect wedding venue.

Elmswood Estate is situated on a higher altitude, which is cooler and thereby allows for late harvesting. The vines put their vigour into the grapes, resulting in a complex, fruit-driven style of wine.

Five Oaks Vineyard

The three-hectare vineyard was established in 1978, and wines produced from the vineyard have won many awards.

It is named Five Oaks after the five magnificent oak trees that grace the property. The vineyard slopes gently westward, overlooking cherry and stone fruit orchards with Mount Dandenong in the background.

Five Oaks specialises in Cabernet Sauvignon, Merlot, Cabernet Sauvignon Merlot and Riesling wines.

Five Oaks is an idyllic setting to enjoy a private event, wedding, wine tasting or function.

Heywood House – Private Garden

Virginia Heywood, host on 3CR's *Gardening Show*, has created a relaxed country garden with outstanding views to the Warburton Ranges. The garden has a number of unusual plants, including *Camellia reticulata*, dogwoods, magnolias, a Judas tree, smoke bushes and *Veltheimia*. A large collection of salvias is flourishing, with help from neighbour Meg Bentley, who has written a book on salvias.

Killara Estate

Killara Estate takes pride in producing the highest-quality wine Victoria can offer. The wines are part of la dolce vita (the good life): good food, good wine and good company. In 1987, the Palazzo family bought the Killara Estate, which, at 485 hectares, is one of the largest private holdings in the valley. Extensive wine tastings, rustic wood-fired Italian produce and outstanding wine selection can all be enjoyed.

In the late 19th century the estate was owned by David Mitchell, father of Dame Nellie Melba, and from 1883 by the legendary David Syme of *The Age* newspaper fame.

McWilliam's Lillydale Estate

McWilliam's is one of Australia's largest and most awarded wineries. The estate has a large function area and restaurant. It is a relaxing place to spend a few hours tranquilly gazing over Mount Toolebewong and the nearby ranges. The vineyard and winery has produced many award-winning wines. Lillydale Estate has been part of the McWilliam's Wine Group since 1994.

Two Brooke's Bar on the estate provides the best of McWilliam's wines, boutique beers and premium

meats cooked to order on the barbecue in the middle of the restaurant.

Paynes Rise

Paynes Rise, a place rich in history, charm and character, is a boutique winery specialising in small batch wines from carefully selected fruit from the vineyard. The cellar door gives visitors the opportunity to wander through the original homestead of Seville's first settler, Thomas Payne.

Paynes Rise wines are a product of exemplary vineyard management and passionate winemaking. The fruit is hand-harvested when fruitfulness, flavour and acidity are in balance, producing cool-climate, boutique wines at their finest.

Thomas Payne built the homestead in 1867. Arriving in Australia in 1852, Payne tried prospecting

in the goldfields for one year, then worked in the building trade. He was granted a 32-hectare allotment in Seville, where he used his skills to construct his home. Unlike other pioneer settlers, he chose general farming rather than fruit-growing.

Seville Estate

Seville Estate is one of Yarra Valley's finest producers. In 1972, Dr Peter McMahon planted the first vines at Seville Estate, as part of the rebirth of the Yarra Valley as a premium wine region. In a region renowned for its red wines from Cabernet and Pinot Noir, it was Seville Estate Shiraz that became

one of Victoria's most sought-after wines.

The estate's wines have been called 'one of Victoria's best kept secrets'. They are some of the most stylish on the market, with vintage tastings showing their superb ageing capacity. Seville Estate also serves fine food in the café-restaurant.

Seville Hill

The Seville Hill estate's long driveway leads past rows of vines, with breathtaking views of the Yarra Valley. Next to the cellar door are beautiful century-old elms. The cellar door has many wine varieties from Sparkling Chardonnay Pinot to a pretty pink Rosé and a range of reds including a Tempranillo. It is set amongst the shade of the English Elms and terraced lawn garden with spectacular views of mountains.

Whispering Hills

Whispering Hills was established in 1985, with vineyard plantings of three hectares within a natural amphitheatre above the township of Seville. Superb wines are produced from hand-picked Riesling, Chardonnay, Pinot Noir, Cabernet Sauvignon and Shiraz. Yields are controlled to enhance quality, and the wines are only released in small quantities.

The cellar door adjoins the boutique winery. In winter, visitors can warm up by the open fire while enjoying a selection of cheeses from the Yarra Valley and France.

Wild Cattle Creek Estate

Wild Cattle Creek Estate is a wonderful location for a wedding or special event with on-site accommodation, estate wines and manicured gardens. Behind 200-year-old doors, the cellar door offers a wide selection of premium wines crafted from the fruit of the vineyard. The menu caters for lunch, dinner or a snack.

Accommodation includes the luxury of the Wallace Historic Homestead in true 19th-century style, to the modern Lotus and Vineyard villas.

STEELS CREEK

Steels Creek was first surveyed in 1839 by Robert Hoddle's assistant, Thomas Nutt, as part of his survey of the Yarra River. Steels Creek is most likely named after early pioneer Michael Steel. Before the district was opened up for settlement, it was part of the Gulf Station squatting run. The 'gold boom' brought people to the area in the 1860s, with nine families listed as residents by 1868. A second boom occurred in the 1890s. Steels Creek is now part of the Yarra Valley winegrowing district.

Brammar Estate

The cellar door opened in early 2005, with a backdrop of natural bushland. Brammar Estate makes white and red wines including unusual blends. All grapes are grown, processed and bottled on the property.

Steels Creek Estate

Established in 1981, the vineyard is situated in the picturesque Steels Creek Valley with views towards Mount Slide and the Kinglake National Park. There is an abundance of wildlife, contributing to the charm of the location. The philosophy of holding back red vintages so they express their bottle age characteristics continues. The Steels Creek Estate style of wine is acknowledged and praised by wine writers and reviewers throughout the world.

TARRAWARRA

Tarrawarra was formerly known as View Hill Estate, when it was owned in 1893 by *The Age* owner and publisher David Syme. Syme gave it the Aboriginal name *Tarrawarra*, which means 'slow waters', describing the bend in the Yarra River. The Tarrawarra railway station opened in 1889 and closed in 1980.

Tarrawarra Abbey

In 1954, Cistercian Monks from Ireland purchased one section of the property comprising 400 hectares, including the large house built by David Syme for his daughter. They established the Tarrawarra Abbey of the Order of Cistercians of the Strict Observance, popularly known as the 'Trappists'.

An avenue of elms leads to Elm Cottage. Today the cottage is used as visitor accommodation.

The monks support themselves by operating a beef herd with Charolais and Red Angus cattle and through Tarrawarra Eucharistic Breads.

The community has added a church, refectory, living quarters, workshops and an extensive library. Life at Tarrawarra Abbey is a contemporary version of ancient Cistercian monasticism, fostering an experience with God and growth in prayer and love.

Elm Cottage

The slab cottage is likely to have been built by William Ryrie in 1839, or in 1850 when Ryrie sold the Yering run and came to live here. It is one of the oldest buildings in Victoria. Richard Robert Woolcott owned the property from 1869 to 1892.

TarraWarra Estate

Since the first vintage over 20 years ago, TarraWarra Estate has established itself as one of Australia's great wine estates, with its Chardonnay and Pinot Noir consistently receiving widespread acclaim and many prestigious Australian and international awards.

At TarraWarra Estate, visitors are invited to reward their senses with the inspired combination of a tasting of fine wines at the cellar door, delicious food in the adjoining restaurant, and wonderful Australian art in a magnificent setting.

TarraWarra Museum of Art

The TarraWarra Museum of Art (TWMA) operates as a not-for-profit institution, with a charter to display Australian art from the second half of the twentieth century to the present day. The TWMA is the first privately funded, significant public visual arts museum set up under the Australian Government's philanthropic measures announced in March 1999.

The TWMA is one of the cultural jewels in the Yarra Valley, providing visitors with an experience comprising stunning architecture and a wealth of modern and contemporary art.

TOOLANGI

Toolangi is an Aboriginal word for 'tall trees'. This area's thick forests of Mountain Ash and Messmate attracted timber cutters and paling splitters in the 1860s. The first land selections took place in the 1880s and many sawmills operated in the early 1900s. The Toolangi primary school was opened in 1895 and the post office, which opened in 1900, was managed by Mrs Bassett for 40 years. The Bassett and the Biggs families were the first to settle in Toolangi in 1894.

Toolangi is an important agricultural area and potatoes have been grown here since the early 1890s. The largest Certified Strawberry Runner Growers' Scheme in the Southern Hemisphere is located in Toolangi. Witlof, bulbs, flowers, berries, grapes and olives are also grown.

Since 1998, Toolangi has been a 'plant protection zone', safeguarding the area from pests and diseases.

The Toolangi Forest Discovery Centre presents information on the forests and history of the area. Walking tracks lead from the centre into the magnificent forest. The tall forests continue to attract bushwalkers and tourists. Wombats, possums, the Black Wallaby, bats, lyrebirds and echidnas live in the area.

So he journeyed to Toolangi,
where the mountain ash yearns skyward,
And the messmate and the blue-gum grow to quite abnormal size.
Spite the 'stately homes' he vaunted,
'twas the simple life he wanted;
And he got it, good and plenty,
at Toolangi on the rise.

C. J. Dennis (1876–1938)

The C. J. Dennis Historic Singing Gardens

Clarence Michael James (C. J.) Dennis (1876–1938), the famous Australian poet and writer who wrote *The Songs of a Sentimental Bloke*, travelled to Toolangi in 1908 with artist Hal Waugh. They camped in tents for three months and Dennis called the tents 'Hall of Hal' and 'Den of Den'.

Dennis bought a 1.4-hectare property in Toolangi in 1915 and named it Arden, which was also known as the 'Singing Garden'. Arden burnt down in 1965, but the garden Dennis created with his wife Olive ('Biddy') — with exotic trees, beautiful rhododendrons, azaleas, pathways and pond — can still be visited. Delicious home-cooked meals and Devonshire teas are available in the tea rooms.

The washhouse is an original building.

English Poet Laureate John Masefield came to Melbourne in 1934 to celebrate the Victorian Centenary. He visited C. J. Dennis at Arden in Toolangi and they planted a Copper Beech tree to commemorate his visit.

Giverny Estate

Giverny Estate, established in the early 1980s, produces sparkling kiwifruit wine, kiwifruit cider, liqueur, kiwi coulis, kiwi jam, chutneys and honey.

A beautiful waterlily pond is reminiscent of Monet's *Water Lilies*, which portrays Monet's garden located at Giverny in France.

My garden is my most beautiful masterpiece.
Claude Monet (1840–1926)

Mount Tanglefoot

The Tanglefoot Walking Track climbs gently along the western slope of Mount Tanglefoot, which is over 1000 metres above sea level. Located in the Toolangi State Forest, it is home to the Powerful and Sooty Owls, Superb Lyrebird, Eastern Whipbird, Rufous and Grey Fantails, and honeyeaters. The track circuits Mount Tanglefoot and climbs to Monda Road, near Mount St Leonard.

Mountain Ash dominates the forest and giant trees over 200 years old can be seen in the rainforest gullies.

Blue Mountain

Blue Mountain in the Toolangi State Forest has views to the Dandenong Ranges and the Yarra Valley. The trail to the summit was a popular horseriding trail in the early 1900s.

A seismic recording station was built by the Australian Government on Blue Mountain in 1962. An underground concrete vault houses the instruments, set into solid rock. This is one of three seismic recording stations in Victoria.

Badham Falls

The falls are thought to have been named after William Henry Badham, who lived in the Toolangi area.

Murrindindi Scenic Reserve

Murrindindi is named after the run taken by Peter Snodgrass, a pastoralist in 1838. *Murrindindi* is derived from an Aboriginal word meaning 'mountain home'. Timber cutters and paling splitters arrived in the late 1800s.

The 815-hectare reserve was established in the Toolangi State Forest in 1981. Mountain Ash, Messmate, Mountain Grey Gums and Myrtle Beech dominate the forest. Wilhelmina Falls and the Murrindindi Cascades are popular destinations.

Wilhelmina Falls

The falls drop 75 metres. Powerful and Sooty Owls, Antechinus, Leadbeater's Possum and Black Wallaby live in the Murrindindi area.

Dindi Mill

The Dindi Mill was built by Fred Corkill and Sam Hansen around 1920 and was one of the largest sawmills in the area.

Murrindindi Cascades

Wirrawilla Rainforest Walk

Wirrawilla is Aboriginal for 'green trees', and the wooden boardwalk that follows Sylvia Creek is accessible by wheelchair.

Myrtle Beech, sassafras, tree ferns and moss grow in the spectacular rainforest. The area is home to one of the world's most entertaining birds, the Superb Lyrebird.

The world's tallest land moss, *Dawsonia superba*

Mount St Leonard

Mount St Leonard is approximately 1000 metres above sea level. The first Mount St Leonard tower was a cabin on top of a sawn-off tree. The cabin was replaced in 1949 by a steel tower that was eventually dismantled, leaving a platform built in 1991 for visitors. Telstra constructed a new tower in 1988 for emergency services, mobile phone networks and fire detection.

Mounts Macedon, Torbreck and Baw Baw, the Strathbogies, Arthurs Seat and Port Phillip Bay can be seen from the panoramic view.

WARBURTON

A settlement was scattered among the mines on the slopes of Mount Little Joe at Yankee Jim's Creek, where gold had been discovered in 1859. 'Yankee Jim' was James McEvoy, a Californian who came to Australia with 'Yankee Ned' (Ned McDonald) to seek their fortunes.

The settlement called Yankee Jim's Creek was renamed Warburton in 1863 in honour of Charles Warburton Carr, the gold warden of the district. It was later changed to Old Warburton when the gold was depleted. During the 1880s, the town on the Yarra River known as Upper Warburton was renamed Warburton.

Timber cutting, sawmills and timber tramways followed. The railway arrived in 1901 and this encouraged tourists to visit and stay in guesthouses.

Seventh-day Adventists moved to Warburton in 1905 and established a publishing business,

health-food factory, school and sanitarium.

In 1954, Queen Elizabeth II and Prince Philip visited by royal train.

The Warburton railway closed in 1965 and is now the Lilydale-to-Warburton Rail Trail, which is popular with walkers, cyclists and horseriders.

Warburton has beautiful views, walking tracks and picturesque picnic spots.

Gainsborough Store

Built in 1909, the Gainsborough Store is the oldest, original store in the district. It was built for E. A. Story and was known as Story's General Provider.

The Rainbow Ice Cream Shop

Waterwheels were used to power goldmines, sawmills and other industries.

Riverside Walk
This five-kilometre scenic walk follows the Yarra River.

Swing Bridge over the Yarra River

Boinga Bob

Boinga Bob builds elaborate temples from a variety of materials.

Warburton Golf Course

An historic smokehouse and dairy (1898), shepherd's hut (1899) and kiln (1899) can be seen near the clubhouse. The club has a picturesque 18-hole, all-weather golf course, with a café and large function centre.

Claremond Cottage – Private Garden

Originally a 0.2-hectare paddock of gum and wattle trees, it is now a beautiful garden. Joe and Barbara Cox, both keen gardeners, transformed the paddock. The garden is a place well worth visiting on the annual Upper Yarra Valley Garden Club Open Weekend.

La-La Falls

Miss Leila Ward, a former landowner, ran a local guesthouse called *La-La*, meaning 'Welcome Welcome'.

The walking track follows Four Mile Creek through the Yarra State Park. Four Mile Creek supplied water to Warburton and, in the 1870s, to the Yarra Yarra Hydraulic Gold Mining Company. The company used hydraulic sluicing to wash soil away and reach the creek beds.

The 1.5-kilometre walk along the remnants of a tramway through luscious forest and giant tree ferns has been popular with tourists since the 1880s.

Wilton Park – Private Garden

Wilton Park is a garden paradise of 1.6 hectares owned by Peter Sexton and David Wilson, who bought the bare land in 2001. It includes rare plants; a Silver Birch grove underplanted with a wide variety of woodland bulbs and plants; a perennial border; Japanese Maples; a subtropical walk including cycads, cool-climate palms and bamboo; and many treasures collected from Tasmania and the Blue Mountains.

View over the Yarra River

Mount Donna Buang

Magistrate Joseph Panton named the mountain 'Acland' in the 1860s but later renamed it 'Donna Buang' after learning the Aboriginal name. Mount Donna Buang's name comes from the Wurundjeri words for 'the body of the mountain'. The mountain rises to a height of 1250 metres and is popular in winter as it is the closest snowfield to Melbourne.

A walking track was cut to the summit in the 1890s. In the 1920s, a 2.4-metre track was established for skiers by the Ski Club of Victoria.

The Brown Wingless Stonefly is found in a one-kilometre area around the summit. There are only two types of Wingless Stonefly in Australia.

The Scarlet Robin (*Petroica boodang*) is at home on Mount Donna Buang.

Lookout Tower

The Lookout Tower was erected shortly after the Donna Buang Bridle Track, from Warburton to the top of Mount Donna Buang, was opened in 1912.

Panoramic views can be enjoyed from the Mount Donna Buang Lookout Tower.

There is nothing in the world more beautiful than the forest clothed to its very hollows in snow. It is the still ecstasy of nature, where every spray, every blade of grass, every spire of reed, every intricacy of twig, is clad in radiance.

William Sharp (1855–1905)

The view from the 10 Mile Picnic Area, where mountain spring water is available in abundance.

Acheron Way

The Acheron Way is a spectacular, historic tourist drive through forests of Mountain Ash and ferns starting from Cement Creek on the Warburton-to-Mount Donna Buang road and continuing to Saint Fillans near Marysville. The Acheron Way was opened in 1929 and reaches an elevation of 832 metres above sea level. Remnants of sawmill sites and views of Mount Donna Buang can be seen.

Acheron River

The Acheron River is 84 kilometres long and flows into the Goulburn River.

Mount Donna Buang Rainforest Gallery

The Rainforest Gallery is located on Mount Donna Buang. Ancient Myrtle Beech up to 400 years old, tall Mountain Ash and luscious ferns and mosses can be seen in the rainforest. Steps from the Skywalk lead to Cement Creek, which flows into the Yarra River.

Cement Creek

Cement Creek is a name from the goldmining era. Miners used this expression to describe the quartz and gravel conglomerates found in the creek.

The Superb Lyrebird can be seen searching for food in the forest.

Shown is one of the two giant Mountain Ash on the Cement Creek walking track. The Mountain Ash is the world's tallest flowering tree and is found only in high-rainfall areas of Victoria and Tasmania.

Mount Donna Buang Skywalk

The Mount Donna Buang Skywalk features a 40-metre-long viewing platform 17 metres above the ground, enabling views through the treetops.

WARBURTON EAST

In 1845, Robert Hoddle's expedition found the source of the Yarra River. The expedition mapped the area and opened the way for fossickers and settlers. Warburton was a mining township around 1865. The road to Warburton terminated there, and packhorses transported provisions from Warburton to the McMahons Creek and Reefton diggings.

Today, there are many wonderful areas that show the history and beauty to the east of Warburton.

The fast-flowing waters of the Yarra River borders the plantation.

California Redwood Plantation

A plantation of approximately 1500 California Redwood (*Sequioa sempervirens*) trees were planted by the Board of Works in 1930. The trees are planted in a grid to study canopy interception in comparison with native trees in the Coranderrk area.

Bishop Pine, Douglas Fir, Radiata Pine, Western Red Cedar and California Redwood trees grow on the plantation.

McMahons Creek

Rich gold reefs were found at the junction of McMahons Creek and the Yarra River in the 1860s. McMahons Creek was a major township in the gold era.

Stepping Stones

These stepping stones are on the track to the Big Peninsula Tunnel. In winter, the water level flows over the stepping stones.

Big Peninsula Tunnel

The river bend was known as the Big Peninsula, since it was a larger bend than that of the Little Peninsula Tunnel. The river was diverted through the tunnel in 1864, but very little gold was extracted from the original river bed. It is 25 metres long.

Little Peninsula Tunnel

In the late 1860s, Chinese miners diverted the course of the Yarra River through a 30-metre-long tunnel. The tunnel was blasted through rock using dynamite, and horse and cart removed the rubble. The miners could then sluice the old stream bed for gold.

O'Shannassy Weir

The weir and aqueduct take their name from the O'Shannassy River, named after three-time premier of Victoria, Sir John O'Shannassy. The O'Shannassy Scheme was constructed between 1911 and 1914, comprising a concrete diversion weir across the O'Shannassy River, and an open aqueduct and pipeline extending 78 kilometres from O'Shannassy Weir to the Surrey Hills Reservoir. The weir and aqueduct were constructed just in time to avert a serious water shortage in Melbourne during the summer of 1914–15.

The aqueduct trail leads to O'Shannassy Weir through the tall Mountain Ash forest.

Shown above is one of the buildings of O'Shannassy Lodge, which was built around 1915 to house Melbourne and Metropolitan Board of Works (MMBW) engineers building the O'Shannassy Dam. It was later transformed into a luxury retreat for MMBW commissioners. Queen Elizabeth II and Prince Philip stayed a few days at the lodge during their 1954 royal visit.

Praise, like gold and diamonds, owes its value only to its scarcity.

Samuel Johnson (1709–1784)

Reefton

During the mid-1860s, large communities of miners lived at the diggings around McMahons Creek and Reefton. In the 1870s, these areas were reworked using sluicing methods. Reefton was a settlement of 3000 miners and their families, but eventually the gold became scarce and the mining camp was abandoned. During the Reefton boom time, there was such an abundance that gold was weighed using ordinary grocer's scales.

Reefton Hotel
The hotel's first owner was Joseph Bowden in 1886. When the gold ran out, Bowden moved the hotel to McMahons Creek.

Upper Yarra Reservoir

The reservoir has a capacity of 200,000 megalitres and is the third-largest of Melbourne's storage reservoirs. The dam wall is 90 metres high, 610 metres long and was completed in 1957. The Upper Yarra Reservoir Park has gardens and picnic grounds, with eucalypt bushland and spectacular scenery.

This is the furthest point upstream on the Yarra River that is accessible to the public.

McVeigh's Waterwheel
McVeigh's Waterwheel once drove the generator to supply power to McVeigh's Hotel, which is now covered by the waters of the Upper Yarra Reservoir. Prior to 1908, the 4.3-metre-tall waterwheel was used at the Contention Mine, ten kilometres to the south-east, and was relocated when mining ceased.

The Fern Gully self-guided trail loops through tall eucalypt forest with a dense, sheltered, ferny understorey. It is home to a number of rare and significant plants and animals, including platypus and Victoria's faunal emblem, the Leadbeater's Possum. Night tours can be arranged to see Greater Gliders, Sugar Gliders, wombats, Swamp Wallabies, possums, bats, Samba Deer and owls.

Yarra Falls

The falls were one of the main tourist attractions along the track starting from McVeigh's Hotel to Mount Baw Baw. The Baw Baw Track was cut in 1907, with huts built for hikers. The falls have a single drop of 25 metres and are located on Falls Creek, with another five waterfalls upstream.

Falls Creek is now in the water catchment area, with no access to Yarra Falls allowed.

Picture from the tourist brochure 'Baw Baw Mountains & past the Yarra Falls. Warburton to Walhalla', c. 1919.

Yankee Jim's Creek

Yankee Jim was a legendary prospector on the Upper Yarra goldfields. He made two large strikes, but squandered his gains and died in poverty at Warrandyte.

There are two similarly named creeks: Yankee Jim's Creek, which flows from Old Warburton to Wesburn; and Little Yankee Jim's Creek, near Reefton. The Yankee Jim Mine, shown right, is one of a number of tunnels near Little Yankee Jim's Creek.

WESBURN

The opening of guesthouses along the Yarra River in the mid-1880s, and a direct road to West Warburton in 1886, foreshadowed the growth of Warburton. There were a number of sawmills in West Warburton, which spurred the opening of the railway in 1901.

By the late 1920s the area had been mostly logged out. In 1925, West Warburton was renamed Wesburn.

The view from Mount Little Joe, which towers above Wesburn and Warburton.

Dolly Grey Park

Dolly Grey Park is located near Scotchman's Creek. 'Goodbye Dolly Grey' was a popular music hall song during the Spanish–American War of 1898 and the Boer War of 1899–1902.

Don't ask what the world needs. Ask what makes you come alive, and go do it. Because what the world needs is people who have come alive.

Howard Thurman (1899–1981)

Historic 1878 miner's cottage

Sam Knott Hotel

The Sam Knott Hotel is one of the district's oldest hotels, previously known as The Warburton Hotel. It was originally located in Old Warburton from about 1864. Edward John Buller (1840–1908) moved the hotel to West Warburton in 1885. The Sam Knott Hotel is named after a prospector who came from England in 1888. In 1906, a photographer snapped Sam drinking at McVeigh's Upper Yarra hotel and sold it to the Carlton Brewery. Sam is famous for his saying, 'I allus has wan at eleven.'

Britannia Creek

Prospectors found gold in the 1850s, with the main rush around 1857–59. The area around the creek was riddled with mine shafts. The official name of the area was Tarrango. A former Royal Navy midshipman, Charles Bowtell, who had served on the *HMS Britannia* during the Crimean War, settled in the valley after being discharged in 1857. Bowtell supported himself by trading in 'spirituous liquors' from a shack named after his ship. The area was soon known as Britannia and the creek as Britannia Creek. Sawmillers moved into the area when the railway was opened in 1901. Later, Cuming, Smith & Co. chose the Britannia locality for a wood distillation works, producing methylated spirits, tar, disinfectants, solvents and axe handles. A sawmill now operates at the site of the Cuming Smith Wood Distillation Plant.

Britannia Creek Falls

The upper falls (left) cascade over boulders. Downstream, Britannia Creek disappears underground and re-appears 150 metres further on from crevices in the rocks.

Britannia Creek Wines

There are four hectares of estate-grown wines, with a variety of vintages available at the cellar door. Vine varietals include Sauvignon Blanc, Chenin Blanc, Semillon, Chardonnay, Merlot, Malbec, Cabernet Franc, Cabernet Sauvignon and Petit Verdot.

Pomberger Farm

Pomberger Farm is an organic farm and garden, operating almost entirely self-sufficiently. It has a comprehensive orchard, vegetable and flower gardens, and a variety of animals.

Pat and Vic Grotaers have been growing organic vegetables and fruit and making cheeses for a number of years.

The Frog Pond

The frogs help control the insects in the garden.

Come forth into the light of things, let nature be your teacher.

William Wordsworth (1770–1850)

WOORI YALLOCK

Five hundred hectares of land near Woori Yallock Creek was gazetted in 1862 as a reserve for Aboriginals who were being forced away from their preferred lands. The Anglo-Saxon population exploring the land for gold forced the Aboriginal population to move to Mohican Station, then to Coranderrk, near Healesville, in 1863. The Woori Yallock post office opened in 1886 as Woori Yalloak, changing its name to Woori Yallock around 1911.

Calulu Park

Joe and Helen Tricarico purchased a bushland lot in 1974, establishing a berry farm, followed in 1982 by a vineyard that has been expanded to seven hectares. Quality wines are crafted, offering excellent value for money. Fresh fruit and produce are also available.

Rayner's Stone Fruit Orchard

Rayner's Stone Fruit Orchard provides quality stone fruit, with over 250 varieties including peaches, nectarines, plums and apricots. Meals are provided in the café, and tractor tours of the orchard are available.

Fruit trees in blossom at Rayner's Stone Fruit Orchard

YARRA GLEN

Yarra Glen was originally known as Yarra Flats. The Ryrie brothers, who arrived in 1837, were the first Europeans to settle in the area, grazing cattle on the Yarra River flats (today known as Chateau Yering). During the 1860s, traders sold provisions to the locals and gold prospectors. A post office was established in 1861 and the railway arrived in 1888. In 1889, Burgoyne and Yarra Flats became the town of Yarra Glen, named after James McPherson's homestead, located downstream. A range of businesses developed including a peg factory, two dairy factories, guesthouses and hotels.

Yarra Glen also became a centre for timber. Horse and bullock teams would transport timber from Toolangi, Kinglake and Steels Creek.

Arthur and Emma Boyd, the parents of esteemed landscape artist Theodore Penleigh Boyd (1890–1923), bought Tralee, a farm in Yarra Glen, where Theodore would paint and sketch on his holidays.

Agriculture, dairying, orchards, sheep and beef farms, wineries and vineyards are located around Yarra Glen today.

View over Alowyn Gardens, Yarra Glen Racecourse and township

The Yarra Glen Station Master lived in a cottage near the railway. The station closed in the early 1980s.

The Colonial Bank of Australasia, built around 1888, was a typical bank of the 1880s boom period. It is now the Hargreaves Hill Brewing Company Restaurant.

A railway trestle bridge crossed the Yarra River, and in the 1880s it was said to be the longest in Australia.

The Grand Hotel was built in 1888 for Mr Farrell to cater for tourists after the opening of the Yarra Glen railway line. The Grand Hotel was known as Farrell's Burgoyne Hotel.

Acacia Ridge

Acacia Ridge has fabulous views of the Great Dividing Range. The vineyard was planted in 1997 and produces affordable, award-winning wines. The Acacia Ridge Miner's Hut is a function room with picturesque views over the winery. Marquees for large events, tours, cellar door sales, barbecue facilities and tastings are also available.

The Miner's Hut, built around 1850, was relocated from the Castlemaine area.

Alowyn Gardens

Alowyn Gardens is an impressive garden of approximately 1.6 hectares designed by Prue and John Van de Linde. It has one of the largest and most spectacular wisteria arbours in Australia. Alowyn Gardens includes a parterre garden, a Silver Birch forest of approximately 500 trees, an edible garden, perennial walk, maple tree courtyard and display gardens. John was named the ABC Gardener of the Year in 2008.

The parterre garden is based on 17th-century French design principles.

Balgownie Estate

Balgownie Estate Vineyard Resort & Spa is ideally situated in the heart of the Yarra Valley, set among the vines with magical views providing the perfect backdrop to any occasion. Exceptional dining, boutique award-winning wines, a luxurious day spa and contemporary suite accommodation are just some of the wonderful things you can enjoy.

Originally chosen for its ideal growing conditions for Chardonnay and Pinot Noir, the vineyard produces a great range of white, red and sparkling wines and maintains a five-star winery rating in James Halliday's *Australian Wine Companion*. The portfolio also includes the original Balgownie Estate collection of cool-climate Shiraz, Cabernet Sauvignon and Chardonnay from the winegrowing region of Bendigo. Wines from both sites are available to taste at the cellar door.

Courtesy of Balgownie Estate

A meeting of birds

Gulf Station

The historically significant Gulf Station is one of Australia's oldest surviving examples of farm buildings constructed from timber slabs in the early 1850s. John Dickson held a grazing lease on the land at Gulf Station around 1844. The property was part of a 10,117-hectare run from Yarra Glen to Toolangi. During the late 1840s, Dickson rented Gulf Station land to Agnes and William Bell, who had arrived from Scotland. In 1851, the discovery of gold enabled the Bells and other farmers to sell food and provisions to gold miners and travellers.

Orchard at Gulf Station

The Gulf Station kitchen included an old colonial oven that was used for baking goods and roasting meat. It stood in the left-hand corner of the fireplace.

The Bells and Thomas Armstrong, a shepherd from Roxborough whom they met on the ship to Australia, took over John Dickson's lease of the run. By 1856, the Bells and Armstrong bought over 500 hectares of Gulf Station land. Clydesdale horses were used for farming, Ayrshire cows were milked, and Border Leicester sheep, Border Leicester–Merino crossbreeds and pigs were bred.

Gulf Station remained in the Bell family until 1951, when it was sold to Jack Smedley and looked after by his sister Ivy Jewson and her husband. Later, Mavis, Jack Smedley's daughter, and her husband, Don Fellowes, managed Gulf Station, where they raised beef cattle and established a nursery.

In 1976, the Victorian Government bought the 16-hectacre property, which is now managed by the National Trust.

Gulf Station School

Lubra Bend – Private Garden

Bordering the Yarra River, Lubra Bend takes its name from a bend in the river where Aboriginal women used to camp. The 120-hectare property was bought in the year 2000 from Margaret Stokes, an experienced gardener. Lubra Bend includes a 1964 Guilford Bell–designed house, japonica and an escallonia double hedge, oak trees and an olive grove. The dry garden and rock pools, designed by Phillip Johnson, feature a cascade flowing into a small billabong and eventually into the Yarra River.

Sticks

Sticks produces premium, award-winning, cool-climate wines that are sold nationally and around the world. Sticks' wines include Chardonnay, Pinot Grigio, Sauvignon Blanc, Pinot Noir, Cabernet Sauvignon and Shiraz as well as the exclusive range of Sticks Yarra Valley No. 29 wines. The picturesque views across the Valley are breathtaking, and its 'cellar door only wines' are produced in boutique batch sizes, available for purchasing.

Train Trak Wines

The train journey from Yarra Glen to Healesville passed through the area now known as the Train Trak vineyard. The family-owned winery of 18 hectares was established in 1995 on a dairy farm. The award-winning wines grown on the estate include Chardonnay, Pinot Noir, Shiraz and Cabernet Sauvignon. The cellar door hosts magnificent 360-degree views of the beautiful Yarra Valley, while the Zonzo Restaurant at the winery provides casalinga-style Italian food.

Yarra Flats Billabongs Reserve

In 1998, the Yarra Flats Billabongs Reserve became Crown Land after Vic Roads changed the Melba Highway at Yarra Glen and built a new bridge over the Yarra River. The billabongs are home to many birds including the Golden-headed Cisticola, Clamorous Reed-warbler, Latham's Snipe, Superb Blue Wren, White-faced Heron, Pacific Black Duck and Purple Swamphen. The reeds, rushes, regionally significant Green-topped Sedge, Swamp Wallaby-grass and 70 species of plants grow around the billabongs, providing creatures a wildlife habitat and safety from predators.

The Battle of Yering

A plaque commemorates the armed conflict at Yering Station, which was owned by William Ryrie. A conflict occurred in January 1840 between 50 Wurundjeri and the Border Police.

Captain Henry Gisborne from Melbourne had been sent by Superintendent Charles Latrobe to apprehend Jaga Jaga, the Wurundjeri leader.

After Jaga Jaga's capture, the Wurundjeri took muskets and spears to rescue their leader imprisoned in the homestead. Shots were fired and the Wurundjeri retreated into the billabong, leading the troopers away from the homestead. Other members of the Wurundjeri then swiftly reached the homestead to rescue their leader.

Yarrawood Estate

Yarrawood Estate is a family-owned vineyard and was established in 1996. The Tall Tales range of estate-grown wines was launched in 2002 with a lyrebird on the label. A large range of multi-award-winning quality red and white wines is available. Perched on top of a hill, the cellar door and café overlook the vineyard.

The mild weather allows for slow ripening and, in combination with restricted yields, leads to production of wines of premium quality.

The property sits at 82–104 metres above sea level.

The beauty of the trees, the softness of the air,

the fragrance of the grass, speaks to me...

And my heart soars.

Chief Dan George (1899–1981)

Yileena Park

Yileena Park is a family-owned vineyard planted with Pinot Noir, Cabernet Sauvignon and Merlot. The wines are highly coloured and have ripe flavours and tremendous depths of character. The unique sandstone cellar door is anchored into a steep hill, ensuring the cool cellaring of its premium wines.

If you want to understand today, you have to search yesterday.
Pearl Buck (1892–1973)

YARRA JUNCTION

Yarra Junction is located at the junction of the Yarra and Little Yarra rivers. It was described as a town in 1901, when it had a telephone office, police station and several shops. The railway station operated on the Warburton line until 1965 and now houses the Upper Yarra Museum.

Yarra Junction was the junction station for the Powelltown Tramway, a three-foot (914-millimetre) gauge railway line that ran between 1913 and 1945. The tramway was owned by the

Powelltown sawmill and transported timber from the mill, tourists and goods. More timber was transported through Yarra Junction than any town in the world except for Seattle (USA).

Blue Lotus Water Garden

Exotic lotuses and waterlilies can be seen on 5.7 hectares of beautifully landscaped gardens established by Geoff and Yvonne Cochrane. The water gardens have two lakes, one of which has ten islands connected by 12 bridges.

Landscaped river flats contain 80 ponds filled with over 50 varieties of lotuses, and three dams display hundreds of flowering waterlilies. Reminiscent of French artist Claude Monet's famous painting series on waterlilies, this garden paradise is spectacular.

Three hothouses display tropical
waterlilies featuring the Charles
Winch Collection.

The slender water lily

Peeps dreamingly out of the lake...

Heinrich Heine (1797–1856)

Giant Amazonian Water Lilies (*Victoria
amazonica*) grow huge circular
leaves over 2.5 metres in diameter.
They originate from South America,
growing in the lakes and backwaters
of the Amazon River.

They were named in honour of
Queen Victoria. A full grown leaf can
support 45 kilograms if the weight is
evenly distributed.

Bulong Estate

With spectacular views of the Yarra Ranges and Mount Donna Buang, the winery, cellar door and restaurant are the perfect place to relax with quality food and wine. Grapes have been grown on the estate since 1995.

Christabel Park – Private Garden

Kathleen and Robert Shelden bought the three-hectare property in 1993. The beautiful garden includes a Cecil Brunner rose hedge taken from cuttings from a bush planted in 1946. A knot garden using *Buxus* (box hedging) is being established.

Upper Yarra Museum

The Upper Yarra Museum displays a magnificent collection of historical memorabilia in an original 1882 railway station. There are other historical buildings including a porter's cottage, goods shed, police station and police cell. A wide range of history is presented, including that of tramways, machinery, gold, photographs and household appliances.

Crank Up

The museum's annual event is Crank Up, which showcases vintage engines and machinery.

YERING

Yering is located between Coldstream and Yarra Glen, and has world-class wineries and restaurants. It is surrounded by rolling fields, vineyards and orchards.

Robert Hoddle surveyed land around Yering in 1838, revealing excellent agricultural country and opening it up for British, Scottish, Irish and Swiss pioneers. Adolphe de Meuron and Paul de Castella purchased a cattle run in Yering, while in 1852 Frederic Guillaume de Pury immigrated to the locale. John Gardiner, the Ryrie family and others farmed sheep and cattle here.

Crop of Brussels sprouts on Yering farmland

Chateau Yering

In 1837, brothers William, Donald and James Ryrie, along with four convict stockmen, departed Monaro in New South Wales, driving 250 head of stock to the Yarra Valley at Yering.

Vine cuttings planted at Yering resulted in Victoria's first vintage in 1845. By 1850 there were over an acre of vines. Paul de Castella, who was to purchase Yering Station, was presented by Donald Ryrie with wine labelled 'Chateau Yering'.

The mansion was constructed in 1854 and was the social centre of the Yarra Valley, with Melbourne socialites staying for weekends.

Aerial view over Chateau Yering
(foreground) and Yering Station

The original house remains intact, with few alterations over the years. The house was completely restored on the inside in 1996 before it opened as a hotel in 1997. The main entrance was originally at the rear where the entrance to the bar from the Sweetwater Café exists.
Courtesy of Chateau Yering

This avenue is approximately one kilometre long, and its 330 elm trees were planted by Paul de Castella for his bride, Lily Anderson.

The gardens were originally laid out in simple form by Donald Ryrie. They were later extended by Paul de Castella with assistance from his friend Baron Ferdinand von Mueller, who in 1857 was director of the Royal Botanic Gardens in Melbourne.

Baron von Mueller planted the Chilean Wine Palm (*Jubaea chilensis*) behind the house in 1867. The two Bunya Pines (*Araucaria bidwillii*) in the front garden were planted around this time and are recorded on the Register of Significant Trees of Victoria. Both the house and the garden are listed by Heritage Victoria.

Coombe Farm

One of the oldest and largest family-owned vineyard estates in the Yarra Valley, Coombe Farm is owned and occupied by the descendants of Dame Nellie Melba.

Coombe Farm is the place for premium viticulture, delicious regional wines and a relaxing Tasting Room experience.

The Oaks – Al Dente Cooking

Located at The Oaks Winery, Al Dente Cooking is a place where friends and family come together to be inspired by rich Italian culture, fresh Yarra Valley produce and Mediterranean cuisine.

An Al Dente Cooking group day is a great way for private or corporate groups to get together in an informal, relaxed environment, and enjoy the fun of a cooking class.

Al Dente Cooking provides traditional hands-on Italian cooking classes and uses fresh local ingredients.

ABOVE
Coombe Farm wines are classically varietal and regionally expressive. They are handcrafted in very small volumes, entirely from estate-grown fruit that has been chosen as the best the vineyard has to offer.

The first wine made under the Coombe Farm label was a Pinot Noir in 2002. Since then, the range has developed into a small yet comprehensive display of both the traditional and alternative varieties that Coombe Farm and the Yarra Valley do best.
Courtesy of Allan Savage

Yarra Valley Dairy

Mary and Leo Mooney started the Yarra Valley Dairy on their dairy farm, Hubertswood, in 1995. Hubertswood is named after the early pioneer Hubert de Castella. The Hubertswood area has a history of dairying, as a cheese factory and a buttery were established here by the early settlers. Yarra Valley Dairy has over 200 cows, which are milked in a herringbone milking shed twice a day. The milk is used in the cheese factory to create the finest quality handmade cheeses, which are sold worldwide. Non-animal rennet is used and the cheese is GM free.

Wine and cheese are complimentary and are brought together by the region's wineries and the Yarra Valley Dairy.

The cheese shop is located in the original 100-year-old milking shed.

Yering Farm

The Deschamps family established the Yering Farm vineyard in the 1800s, when it was known as the Yeringa Vineyard. Old farm gates and grain silos are reminders of the cellars that once stood on the property.

The Johns family acquired the 80 hectares of prime farming land in 1980 and replanted the first grape vines in 1989. The estate is focused on producing high-quality fruit across each of the grape varieties. Wine production is carefully controlled by Alan Johns.

Alan handcrafts original New World wines from estate-grown fruit. Yering Farm produces wonderfully soft and elegant examples of the Yarra Valley's premium, cool-climate wines.

For over 150 years, the rich loam soil of the Yeringa vineyard has produced exceptional wines, which won awards over a century ago and continues to do so today. Wines under the Yering Farm label have received glowing reviews on the wine circuit, winning numerous awards and recognition in the industry.

Fruit Trees
Premium seasonal fruit is grown on the farm.

Yering Farm Cellar Door
The old hay shed situated at the top of the hill overlooks stunning views and has been converted into a cellar door with old-world charm.

Yering Gorge Cottages

Yering Gorge Cottages is set on 44 hectares of nature reserve located on the banks of the Yarra River. Self-contained luxury accommodation is available in modern cottages. There is abundant wildlife in the area, with kangaroos, as well as echidna, wombats, wild deer, koalas and possums.

John & Joseph Furphy

Joseph Furphy (184–1912) was the first Caucasian child born in the Yarra Valley. His father, Samuel Furphy, emigrated in 1841 from Ireland to Australia. Samuel was the head gardener at Yering Station, where Joseph was born. The Furphy family later relocated to a number of towns in central Victoria and to Western Australia.

Joseph was a farmer at Kyneton and Colbinabbin, and later a carter of goods with his own bullock team in the Riverina area of New South Wales. In 1884, Joseph worked with his brother John in his iron foundry in Shepparton.

Over the years, Joseph concentrated on reading and his writing. He wrote with great moral passion and is regarded as the 'Father of the Australian Novel'. Writing under the pseudonym Tom Collins, his novel *Such is Life* is considered an Australian classic.

Joseph was known to be kind-hearted, lived by the teaching that the love of money is the root of all evil, and counselled intemperate men.

John Furphy (1842–1920) was Joseph's older brother, born at Kangaroo Ground. He worked as a blacksmith at Kyneton and later Shepparton, where his business expanded into iron-founding. Producing agricultural implements, he made a grain-stripping machine, furrow plough and iron swingletrees. However, John's most famous product was an 818-litre cylindrical iron tank drawn by horse on a wooden frame with cast-iron wheels. Known as 'Furphies', these water-carts were used on farms and in large numbers during World War I. When soldiers gathered around the water-carts, they became sites for gossip, leading the word 'furphy' to eventually mean 'a false report'. An estimated 300 water-carts were produced annually for 40 years.

It is appropriate that inscribed on the metal end of each cart were the following words:

Good . Better . Best.
Never let it rest.
Till your Good is Better
And your Better – Best.

Yering Station

Yering Station is a family-owned winery producing award-winning wines of world-class quality and distinction. It was Victoria's first vineyard, planted by the Ryrie brothers in 1838 who named the property *Yering*, Aboriginal for 'a deep pool' and 'a watering and gathering place'. The Ryries planted two grape varieties: the 'Black Cluster of Hamburg' and a white grape variety called 'Sweetwater'. During the early 1850s they returned to Sydney and Paul de Castella took ownership of Yering Station, developing the property from primarily a cattle station into a premier winery. In 1889, Yering Station won the Grand Prix at the Universal Exhibition in Paris. Only 14 such awards were ever granted internationally.

Yering Station was purchased in 1996 by the Rathbone family. Melbourne architect Robert Conti designed the

Yering Station hosts art and sculpture exhibitions and the Yarra Valley Regional Farmers' Market.
The popular farmers' market is held in the historic barn on the third Sunday of each month.

The cellar door was established in 1859.

state-of-the-art complex where visitors can enjoy the full range of Yering Station wines. The Wine Bar Restaurant, with its breathtaking views over the Yarra Valley, has tempting menus using fresh, seasonal, local produce.

YERINGBERG

Yeringberg was established in 1863 by Baron Frederic Guillaume de Pury (1831–1890), who emigrated from Switzerland. He bought land from Paul de Castella's Yering cattle station. Baron de Pury and his son George made Yeringberg renowned in the wine world. Most of the Yeringberg wine was exported to London. Wines were produced until 1921, winning gold medals in London, Paris, Bordeaux, Brussels, Calcutta and San Francisco, as well as many prizes in Australia. In 1921, Yeringberg was the last winery to pull out their vines. The decline of the world market, the starlings and the downy mildew led to the demise of the Yarra Valley vineyards.

In 1969, third-generation winegrower Guill de Pury re-established the vineyard on the slopes originally chosen by his grandfather. The de Pury family now produce 1500 cases of wine each year from some of the oldest vines in the Yarra Valley. The wine is made only from grapes grown at Yeringberg.

Guill and his daughter Sandra are the winemakers, and the wine is cellared in the best French oak barrels. Guill's son David is the viticulturist and farm manager, while Katherine, who is married to Guill, assists with the marketing.

Yeringberg vines

Yeringberg makes six different wines: Chardonnay, Marsanne/Roussanne, Viognier, Pinot Noir, Shiraz and Yeringberg (a Cabernet blend).

Today, Yeringberg is a mixed farming property of 485 hectares with 2000 sheep and their lambs, 250 cattle and vineyards.

The stables were constructed around 1885.

Historic Winery

The original two-storey, wooden winery was built by David Mitchell. Built between 1865 and 1895 on foundation stones quarried from the property, the unique winery is of historical and architectural significance. The winery is unchanged, has substantial underground cellars, and is listed by the National Trust.

The first floor was supported by uniquely designed roof trusses. The buggy used by Sandra and David de Pury's grandmother, and equipment used in 19th-century winemaking, can be viewed in the winery.

The grapes were crushed on the top floor in wooden containers. These were pushed along rail tracks and their contents tipped into the press or the fermenting vats. A steam engine was used to power a lift in the winery.

Two large cellars continue to be used today. Yeringberg operates a cellar door one weekend in May each year, when new vintage wines are released to customers on the mailing list.

ACKNOWLEDGMENTS

Thank you to all the people who assisted in the creation of this book. In particular, we would like to thank the following people and those who choose to remain anonymous.

Al Fencaros – Allinda Winery
Alex Hill – Coldstream Hills
Ali – Healesville Blueberry Farm
Anda & David Crothers – Brumfield Winery
Bert Rijk – The Big Bouquet
Bob & Kathleen Sheldon – Christabel Park
Bob Curtis – Yileena Park Vineyard
Brett Butcher – Soumah
Brett Morton – Yarra Valley Railway
Bridie Flynn – Pictures Collection, State Library of Victoria
Bruno Torfs – Bruno's Art & Sculpture Garden
Cassandra O'Brien – The National Trust of Australia (Victoria)
Chantelle Eve – Balgownie Estate
Cheryl Phillips – Bollygum Adventure Park
Danny Kane – Oakridge
David Tomlins – Tarrawarra Abbey
Deanne & Toby Eccles – Strathvea Guesthouse
Di Logg – Yarra Valley Dairy
Fiona Johnston – Dalblair
Gavan Oakley – Acacia Ridge
Geoff & Yvonne Cochrane – Blue Lotus Farm
Geoff Durham – Wanderslore Sanctuary
Georgie & Will Leckey – Two Rivers Green Tea Plantation
Graeme Miller – Miller's Dixons Creek Estate
Greg Jarratt – St Huberts
Han Tao Lau – Long Gully Estate
Helen & Joe Tricarico – Calulu Park
Ian Simmonds – Archery Park
Jan Williams – Singing Gardens Tea Room
Janine Hallas – Warramate Wines, Yarra Yering
Jenny & Leslie Dovaston – Marysville Trout & Salmon Ponds
Joe & Barbara Cox – Claremond Cottage
Joe & Maryanne Messina – The Hermitage
John Knoll – Healesville Contemporary Art Space & Palate, Mt Rael
Joy Wandin-Murphy – Senior Wurundjeri Elder
Judy & Wally Zuk – Five Oaks Vineyard
Kath Hemer – Fergusson Winery

Katrina Reynolds – Immerse
Keith Johnson – Upper Yarra Museum
Kerrie Lyons – TarraWarra Estate
Kevin – Killara Park Estate
Lea – Hedgend Maze
Leanne De Bortoli – De Bortoli Yarra Valley Estate
Len Rayner – Rayner's Stonefruit Orchard
Leon and Rita Tokar – Tokar Estate
Lorraine Hunter – Giverny Estate
Lynne Mc Call – Yarra Valley Herb Farm & Redgum Gallery
Max Petronio – Yering Farm
Maxine Briggs – Koori Liaison Officer, State Library of Victoria
Merilyn Wheatfill – Providence Ponds
Michael Gelbert – Buxton Ridge Winery
Michael Hibbert – Warburton Golf Club
Mitch MacRae – Buxton Trout & Salmon Farm
Myrtle & John Nolan – Nolan Winery
Nicole Esdaile – Coombe Farm
Nikki Casey – The Big Berry
Olwyn & Manfred Scharley – Tall Timbers
Patty & Victor Grotaers – Pomberger Farm
Peter & Trish Boerlage – Magic Garden Roses
Peter Doyle – Haining Farm
Peter Sexton, David Wilson – Wilton Park
Prue & John Van de Linde – Alowyn Gardens
Ron Phelan – Sutherland Estate
Rosemary Simpson – Lubra Bend
Ross Stevens – Yerring Gorge Cottages
Sandra de Pury – Yeringberg
Simone Bannister – Domaine Chandon
Stephanie Cooksey – Elmswood Estate
Sue O'Brien – Chateau Yering
Tim Cullen – Paynes Rise
Tim Schwaiger – Yarrawood
Turid Shanmugam – Shantell Vineyard & Winery
Virginia Heywood – Heywood House

DIRECTORY

AREA	PLACE OF INTEREST	MELWAY REF.	WEBSITE
Acheron	Two Rivers Green Tea Plantation, 150 Connellys Creek Rd	910 S8	www.tworiversgreentea.com.au/the-tea-shop
Black Spur	Boat O'Craigo, 458 Maroondah Hwy	270 J11	www.boatocraigo.com.au
	Condon's Track	270 J7	
	Fernshaw Park	10 R4	
	Graceburn Weir	10 R4	
	Maroondah Reservoir Park	270 K11	
	Mount Dom Dom	10 R3	
	Mount Juliet	10 R4	
	Old Black Spur Road	10 R3	
	Saint Ronan's Well	10 R3	
Bunyip State Park	Four Brothers Rocks	14 R12	
Buxton	Buxton Ridge Winery, 88 Seal Rock Rd	910 T10	
	Buxton Silver Gum Reserve	910 T10	
	Buxton Trout & Salmon Farm, 2118 Maroondah Hwy	910 T10	
Cathedral Ranges	Cathedral Ranges State Park	910 T10	
Christmas Hills	Bend of Islands	279 B2	
	Sugarloaf Reservoir	273 B2	
Coldstream	Badger's Brook Estate, 874 Maroondah Hwy	277 B9	www.badgersbrook.com.au
	Domaine Chandon, 727 Maroondah Hwy	276 D8	www.domainechandon.com.au
	Dominique Portet, 870–872 Maroondah Hwy	277 A9	www.dominiqueportet.com
	Gateway Estate, 669 Maroondah Hwy	281 A7	http://gatewayestate.com.au
	Helen's Hill Estate, 16 Ingram Rd	281 D11	www.helenshill.com.au
	Maddens Rise, Maddens Lane	276 K11	www.maddensrise.com
	Maroondah Orchards, 713–719 Maroondah Hwy	276 A11	
	Oakridge, 864 Maroondah Hwy	276 J9	www.oakridgewines.com.au
	Punt Road, 10 St Huberts Rd	275 J12	www.puntroadwines.com.au
	Rochford, cnr Maroondah Hwy & Hill Rd	277 D9	www.rochfordwines.com.au
	St Huberts, cnr Maroondah Hwy & St Huberts Rd	275 K12	www.sthuberts.com.au
	Stones, 14 St Huberts Rd	275 H11	www.stonesoftheyarravalley.com
	Tokar Estate, 6 Maddens Lane	276 K10	www.tokarestate.com.au
Dixons Creek	Allinda Winery, Lorimers Lane	10 P3	www.allindawinery.com.au
	De Bortoli Yarra Valley Estate, Pinnacle Lane	10 P3	http://debortoliyarra.com.au
	Fergusson Winery, Wills Rd	267 G1	www.fergussonwinery.com.au
	Immerse, 1548 Melba Hwy	267 K1	www.immerseyourself.com.au
	Mandala, 1568 Melba Hwy	267 K1	http://mandalawines.com.au
	Miller's Dixons Creek Estate, 1620 Melba Hwy	267 K1	www.graememillerwines.com.au
	Shantell Vineyard & Winery, 1974 Melba Hwy	10 P3	www.shantellvineyard.com.au
	Sutherland Estate, 2010 Melba Hwy	10 P3	http://sutherlandestate.com.au
Gruyere	Coldstream Hills, 31 Maddens Lane	283 A6	www.coldstreamhills.com.au
	Medhurst Wines, 24–26 Medhurst Rd	282 J7	http://medhurstwines.com.au
	Soumah, 18 Hexham Rd	277 G12	http://soumah.com.au
	Warramate Hills	285 G1	
	Warramate Wines, 27 Maddens Lane	283 A6	www.warramatewines.com.au
	Yarra Yering, 4 Briarity Rd	283 A4	www.yarrayering.com
Healesville	Badger Weir Park	10 R5	
	Blueberry Farm, 11 Garnook Grove	278 H10	http://blueberrywinery.com.au
	Coronation Park	270 C12	
	Donnelly's Weir	270 G6	
	Giants Steps / Innocent Bystander Winery, 336 Maroondah Hwy	270 D12	www.innocentbystander.com.au
	Healesville Contemporary Art Space & Palate, Basement, 177–179 Maroondah Hwy	278 B1	http://hcas.com.au/
	Healesville Sanctuary, Badger Creek Rd	278 F8	www.zoo.org.au/HealesvilleSanctuary
	Hedgend Maze, 163 Albert Rd	278 F6	www.hedgend.com.au
	Lake Yumbunga, Healesville–Kinglake Rd	269 J6	
	Long Gully Estate, Long Gully Rd	270 D10	http://longgullyestate.com
	Magic Garden Roses, 77 Healesville–KooWeeRup Rd	278 B7	www.magicgardenroses.com.au

AREA	PLACE OF INTEREST	MELWAY REF.	WEBSITE
	Meyers Creek Falls, Myers Creek Rd	270 D1	
	Mount Rael, 140 Healesville–Yarra Glen Rd	269 F12	http://mtrael.com.au/
	Mount Riddell	10 R5	
	Nolan Winery, 217 Badger Creek Rd	278 J9	www.nolanvineyard.com.au
	Queens Park	270 D12	
	Riverstone Estate, Skye Rd	277 F10	www.riverstonewine.com.au
	Strathvea Guesthouse, 755 Myers Creek Rd	10 Q3	http://strathvea.com.au/
	The Big Bouquet, Barak Lane	278 B9	www.bigbouquet.com.au
	The Slow Coach Dining Carriage		www.slowcoach.com.au
	Tourist Information Centre	278 B1	www.visityarravalley.com.au
	Yarra Valley Railway, Healesville Station, Healesville–Kinglake Rd	278 A1	www.yarravalleyrailway.org.au
Hoddles Creek	The Big Berry, 925 Gembrook Rd	14 R9	www.thebigberry.com.au
Kinglake	Bollygum Adventure Park, 40 Whittlesea–Kinglake Rd	380 E9	www.bollygumpark.org.au
	Jehoshaphat Valley	380 H12	
	Lady Stonehaven's Lookout	10 B8	
	Wombelano Falls, Captains Creek Rd	910 P11	
Launching Place	Archery Park, Don Rd	287 H5	www.yarravalleyarcherypark.com.au
	Home Hotel	287 H6	www.thehomehotel.com
Lilydale	Anglican Church of St John the Baptist, cnr Jones & Castella Sts	38 F3	
	Bianchet Winery, 187 Victoria Rd	280 C6	www.bianchetwinery.com.au
	Lillydale Lake	38 F6	
	Lilydale and District Historical Society, 61 Castella St	38 F4	www.lilydalehistorical.com.au
	Mechanics Institute Athenaeum and Free Library, 39–41 Castella St	38 F4	
	Melba Park, Chapel St	38 F4	
	Yarra Valley Herb Farm, 2 Victoria Rd	38 B5	www.lilydaleherbfarm.com
Marysville	Bruno's Art & Sculpture Garden	910 T11	www.brunosart.com
	Cambarville, Cumberland Falls	912 U1	
	Keppel's Hut	910 U11	
	Lady Talbot Drive	910 T11	
	Lake Mountain	910 U11	
	Marysville Trout & Salmon Ponds, 261 Marysville Rd	910 T11	www.marysvilletrout.com.au

AREA	PLACE OF INTEREST	MELWAY REF.	WEBSITE
	Steavenson Falls	910 T11	
	The Big Culvert	910 U11	
Millgrove	Dee Split Bridge	289 C1	
	Platts Falls	10 R7	
Mount Donna Buang	10 Mile Picnic Area	912 S2	
	Acheron Way	912 S1	
	Cement Creek Rainforest Gallery	912 T2	
	Lookout Tower	912 S2	
Narbethong	The Hermitage, 161 Maroondah Hwy	912 S1	www.thehermitage.net.au
Noojee	Amphitheatre & Toorongo Falls	912 V4	
	Trestle Bridge	912 V4	
Panton's Gap	Ben Cairn, Malleson's Glen	912 S2	
	Malleson's Lookout, Mount Toolebewong	912 R2	
Powelltown	Ada No 2 Mill, Ada Tall Trees Reserve, Big Rock	912 U3	
	Gilderoy Falls	912 S4	
	Mount Myrtalia	912 T3	
	Seven Acre Rock	912 T4	
	Starlings Gap	912 P3	
	The Bump	912 T4	
Rubicon	Fifteen Thousand Foot Siphon Trestle Bridge	910 U10	
	Mount Torbreck	910 T9	
	Rubicon Falls	910 U10	
	Snobs Creek Falls, Snobs Creek Fish Hatchery	910 U8	
Seville	Ainsworth Estate, Ducks Lane	285 D12	www.ainsworth-estate.com.au
	Brumfield Winery, 539 Queens Rd	121 D3	www.brumfield.com.au
	Carriage Café	119 J8	www.carriagecafe.com.au
	Dalblair, 65 Ducks Lane	285 12C	www.dalblairbnb.com.au
	Elmswood Estate, 75 Monbulk–Seville Rd	305 C6	www.elmswoodestate.com.au
	Five Oaks Wines, 60 Aitken Rd	305 A6	www.fiveoaks.com.au
	Killara Park Estate, cnr Warburton Hwy & Sunnyside Rd	285 G9	www.killaraestate.com.au
	McWilliams Lillydale Estate, 45 Davross Ct	305 F1	www.mcwilliams.com.au

AREA	PLACE OF INTEREST	MELWAY REF.	WEBSITE
	Paynes Rise, 10 Paynes Rd	119 J11	www.paynesrise.com.au
	Seville Estate, 65 Linwood Rd	305 C1	www.sevilleestate.com.au
	Seville Hill, 8 Paynes Rd	119 J11	www.sevillehill.com.au
	War Memorial Park	119 K11	
	Whispering Hills, 580 Warburton Hwy	119 H11	www.whisperinghills.com.au
	Wild Cattle Creek, cnr Warburton Hwy & Wallace Rd	119 F11	www.wildcattlecreek.com.au
Steels Creek	Brammar Estate, 583 Steels Creek Rd	10 P3	www.brammarestatewinery.com.au
	Steels Creek Estate, 1 Sewell Rd	10 P3	www.steelsckestate.com.au
Tarrawarra	Tarrawarra Abbey, 659 Healesville–Yarra Glen Rd	276 G2	www.cistercian.org.au
	TarraWarra Estate, 311 Healesville–Yarra Glen Rd	277 B2	www.tarrawarra.com.au
Toolangi	Badham Falls, Blue Mountain	10 Q2	
	Dindi Mill Site	910 R10	
	Giverny Estate, 69 Cherrys Lane	10 Q2	www.givernyestate.com
	Mount St Leonard	10 Q3	
	Mount Tanglefoot	10 Q1	
	Murrindindi Cascades	910 R10	
	Singing Gardens Tea Room, 1694 Main Rd	10 Q2	www.yarravalleynow.com.au/singing-gardens
	Sylvia Creek Falls	10 Q2	
	Wilhelmina Falls	910 R10	
	Wirrawilla Rainforest Walk	10 Q2	
Warburton	Golf Club	289 J4	www.warburtongolf.com.au
	La-La Falls	290 F10	
	Mount Little Joe	289 G7	
	Riverside Walk	290 D4	
	Sanitarium Health Food Company	290 D4	www.sanitarium.com.au
	Signs Publishing Company	290 D4	http://signspublishing.com.au
Warburton East	Big Peninsula Tunnel	912 U2	
	Californian Redwood Plantation	291 F2	
	Little Peninsula Tunnel	292 J1	
	McVeigh's Waterwheel	912 U2	
	O'Shannassy Weir	912 T2	
	Reefton Hotel, Upper Yarra Reservoir	912 U2	

AREA	PLACE OF INTEREST	MELWAY REF.	WEBSITE
Wesburn	Britannia Creek Caves & Falls	10 S8	
	Britannia Creek Winery, 75 Britannia Creek Rd	10 S8	
	Dolly Grey Park	289 K5	
	Sam Knott Hotel	289 B7	www.samknotthotel.com.au
Woori Yallock	Calulu Park, 1800 Warburton Hwy	306 K2	
	Rayner's Stonefruit Orchard, 60 Schoolhouse Rd	306 K5	www.raynerstonefruit.com.au
Yarra Glen	Acacia Ridge, 169 Gulf Rd	267 C6	www.acaciaridgeyarravalley.com
	Alowyn Gardens, 1210 Melba Hwy	267 G9	www.alowyngardens.com.au
	Balgownie Estate, 1309 Melba Hwy	267 G7	http://balgownieestate.com.au
	Gulf Station, 1029 Melba Hwy	267 C11	www.gulfstation.com.au
	Railway Station	274 K2	
	Roundstone Winery & Vineyard, 54 Willow Bend Drive	10 P4	
	Sticks Yarra Valley, 179 Glenview Rd	274 F2	www.sticks.com.au
	Train Trak Vineyard, 957 Healesville–Yarra Glen Rd	275 F3	www.traintrak.com.au
	Yarra Flats Billabongs Reserve	275 A3	
	Yarrawood Estate, 1275 Melba Hwy	267 F7	www.yarrawood.com.au
	Yileena Park Vineyard, 245 Steels Creek Rd	266 K5	www.yileenapark.com.au
Yarra Junction	Blue Lotus Farm, 2628 Warburton Hwy	288 H8	www.bluelotusfarm.com.au
	Bulong Estate, 70 Summerhill Road	288 G12	http://Bulongestate.com.au
	Upper Yarra Museum, Melba Hwy	288 D7	http://upperyarramuseum.org.au
Yering	Chateau Yering, 42 Melba Hwy	275 B5	www.chateauyering.com.au
	Coombe Farm, 11 St Huberts Rd	275 H12	www.coombefarm.com.au
	The Oaks Winery – Al Dente Cooking	281 B1	www.aldentecooking.com.au
	Yarra Valley Dairy, 70–80 Meikans Rd	275 C10	www.yvd.com.au
	Yering Farm, St Huberts Rd	275 E11	www.yeringfarmwines.com.au
	Yering Gorge Cottages	273 K11	www.yeringcottages.com.au
	Yering Station, 38 Melba Hwy	275 C6	www.yering.com
Yeringberg	Yeringberg	276 D10	www.yeringberg.com